BEING
HUMAN BEING

Praise for the Book

Being Human Being points to the fact that the world's peoples have work to do to become what we were all meant to be from the beginning, and the fact that we have lost our collective humanity in pursuit of a fleeting illusion and that we have to find our way back to our authentic identity as human beings. The authors argue that there is a need to rescue how we think and talk about race/racism to win back ourselves for the good of all, including the perpetrators and beneficiaries of racism.

From my conversation with the authors about this book and their many other works that I have read, Dr. Asante and Dr. Dove are not just professors but sages at whose feet America should sit for instruction more than it is currently doing. Reading this book is coming face to face with Afrocentric genius, wisdom and cutting-edge intellectual competence that has made the authors the household names that they are in Africology.

—Tavengwa Gwekwerere, PhD
College of Ethnic Studies, Department of Pan-African Studies
California State University, Los Angeles, CA

Molefi Kete Asante and Nah Dove challenge the reigning discourses about race in their new book, *Being Human Being: Transforming the Race Discourse*. They are not content merely to further debunk the false notion of race as a biological term, but they argue that the imaginary racial ladder that maintains so much of the discourse about race must be identified and taken down.

—Carol A. Blackshire-Belay, PhD
Vice President of Institutional Effectiveness
Rocky Vista University, Parker, CO

There are hundreds of works that explore race as a social construct that correctly problematizes its development. *Being Human Being: Transforming the Race Discourse* takes it much further. First, it is uniquely an Afrocentric exploration of the artificial construct. It places Africans at the center of humanity and African culture as the ultimate representation of what it means to be human. It reframes the discussion of race as a discussion of human categories, or human cultures; cultural constructs rather than racial ones.

—Adisa A. Alkebulan, PhD
Chair & Associate Professor
Department of Africana Studies
San Diego State University, San Diego, CA

BEING HUMAN BEING

Transforming the Race Discourse

MOLEFI KETE ASANTE AND NAH DOVE
Temple University

W• Universal Write Publications, LLC
New York, New York

No part of this publication may be reproduced in whole or in part, or stored in a retrieval system, or transmitted in any form or by any means, electronic, mechanical, photocopying, recording, or otherwise, without written permission from the publisher, except in the case of newspapers, magazines, and websites using quotations embodied in critical essays and reviews.

BEING HUMAN BEING
Transforming the Race Discourse

Copyright © 2021 Universal Write Publications, LLC
All rights reserved.

Mailing/Submissions:
Universal Write Publications, LLC
421 8th Avenue, Suite 86
New York, NY 10116
Website: www.UWPBooks.com

ISBN: 978-1-942774-09-9

This book has been published with the support of Sage Publishing

Contents

Dedication .... *vi*
Author Biographies .... *vii*
Acknowledgments .... *viii*
Preface .... *ix*
Introduction 1

CHAPTER 1
   Patriarchy: The Origin of Hierarchy and Race. 13
CHAPTER 2
   Race and Culture. 53
CHAPTER 3
   The Illusive Nature of Race. 89
CHAPTER 4
   The Promoters of Racism 117
CHAPTER 5
   Beyond Race: The Quest Back to Humanity 153

Index 211

DEDICATED TO

We dedicate this book to our children, grandchildren, and great grandchildren: MK, Eka, Mario, Jamar, Ayaana, Nova, Akila, Akira, Aion, Siona Ankrah, Nadu, Alistair Akintoye, Olatunju, Akua, Hope, Adjowa, Abena, Nia, Otis, Des, Kwabena, Rochelle, Layla, Lani, Elijah, Kymani, and Yaa.

May they continue the search for humanity as we defeat race, notions of group superiority based on false claims for privilege, and special treatment by society.

Author Biographies

Molefi Kete Asante received his doctorate from the University of California, Los Angeles, and teaches at Temple University in the Department of Africology. His books include *The History of Africa*, *Erasing Racism: The Survival of the American Nation*, and *Radical Insurgencies*.

Nah Dove received her doctorate from the State University of New York at Buffalo, and teaches Afronography, the Black Woman, and Afrocentric Education at Temple University in the Department of Africology. Her books include *Afrikan Mothers: Bearers of Culture, Makers of Social Change* and *The Afrocentric School*.

Acknowledgments

We have written this book together, but we have not written it alone. Our enablers have been colleagues, friends, and family and sometimes strangers that we met on our journey of life. Our influences are many, too many to truly name in full, but we especially give praise to Cheikh Anta Diop, Frances Cress Welsing, Abdias do Nascimento, Dani Nabudere, Toyin Falola, Joyce King, Ivan Van Sertima, Ifi Amadiume, Maat Ka-Re-Monges, Asa Hilliard, and those who stood beside them whom we may never know.

Ayo Sekai of UWP and Geane de Lima of Sage Publishing have rescued us from the depths many times and we owe both sincere gratitude for wisdom and guidance. Ayo Sekai, UWP's leader, recognized our passion for this project and advanced it to her editorial advisors for which we are pleased. In addition, we appreciate the support of Reynaldo Anderson, editorial board chair, for urging the publication of this manuscript.

We wrote this book, but it is in partnering with a prolific African-centered publishing company that made it better. We are in awe of Universal Write Publications, and the team that made this book possible. We are beholden to our students at Temple University for their inquiring minds, debating skills, and critical inquiries into the nature of racism in the American society.

Preface

Social change can be slow, but it always responds to agitation. *Being Human Being* is a narrative agitation with a fresh examination of state of the discourse around the illusions of race. We began this work with the intent to transform race discourses so that we slow the pace on debating illusions and rather spend our time nudging the human community toward the idea of humanity. Thus, our subtitle is *Transforming the Race Discourse*, which speaks to the need to escape the entrapment of race itself. The falsity of race in biological terms has been demonstrated for decades now, yet it persists, and many of us have been participants, in the language of racial relations, race interactions, and racial disparities as a way of promoting the idea of a false reality. We live and die by its very terms. Hundreds of millions of us have been wiped off the face of the earth. Can we come to our senses? We believe that we can, in time, but there is no time like the present to make social change.

At the very dawn of *Homo sapiens* on the vast African plains, the first humans established the behaviors that would assist them in regulating how we react to one another in different situations. As scientists they worked out the movements of the planets, the impact of nature on our ability to live, they laid the groundwork mapping areas of land and buildings astronomically precise. We are still working out their contribution to our knowledge development and yet our ancestors are still ranked as primitive.

It would be millennia before humans would devise ways to find differences and rank them to erode the notion of humans existing as a common group. While some believe the increasing diversity of humanity may have caused ranking of difference, it is more likely that the overthrow of African matriarchy, the peaceful coexistence of women and men, and the resulting consequences of authorial power of religious doctrines entrenched in our imagination birthed our current cultural conflicts.

We know historically that rulers of nations have come in all colors and genders, and that Menes, the first nation-builder, was a black African man from the Nile River Valley, and that Sobrenefru, a black woman, was the first significant queen leader in history. However, we also know that in India, Southwest Asia, and Europe, blackness, whether male or female, took on negative implications in religions. Icons and symbols representing good and evil, high and low, were often correlated in the minds of those who constructed these religions with light and darkness. Race was easily advanced as a concept to capture what was already circulating in the narratives of power in Europe and Asia. Nowhere in African culture was this myth of race at work in the way we have found it in the Western imagination.

It would not be long before the so-called Age of Discovery and Enlightenment Period firmly implanted this ideology of race in the minds of Europeans. Among Asians, it would be the *varnas*, a term like race, and similarly implanted in the imagination of people, which divided humans because of complexion and color. Thus, the racial ladder as we call it was an imaginary hierarchical arrangement which ranked humans according to negative and positive traits correlated with color. Our objective has been to question this racial ladder and to seek a return to the source: the African idea of humanity. What is most human is the quest for Maaticity, that is, the attainment of truth, justice, righteousness, harmony, balance, order, and reciprocity. Therefore, we say *Being Human Being: Transforming the Race Discourse* agitates for an overturning of race in our language and the assertion of a language of seeking humanity, that is, Maaticity.

Introduction

In a very telling passage in his popularly acclaimed book *How to Be an Antiracist*, Ibram Kendi (2019), the brilliant writer, asks a question and makes statements in this vein:

> What's the problem with being "not racist"? It is a claim that signifies neutrality: "I am not a racist, but neither am I aggressively against racism." But there is no neutrality in the racism struggle. The opposite of "racist" isn't "not racist." It is "antiracist." (p. 9)

Kendi is right to see "racist" not merely as descriptive but also as pejorative. Our objective is to go even further and to proclaim that only an end to the language of race itself can solve the problem of racism.

Our book is about social transformation of an illusory concept that has penetrated domestic and international space since its beginning in the deep trenches of religious and mythological thought. Propagated by the various engines of communication—war, insults, projection, rote memory, symbols, coats-of-arms, medallions, and writing—this race illusion has become the bane of the international order. For centuries, the European cultural expression has been wrapped in the fabrics of this invention and has spread its cover worldwide. But Europe is neither the first nor the only promoter of this racial idea; it is perhaps the most efficient and the source of the greatest crimes against humanity based on this false doctrine of segmenting the human population on the basis of ranked categories. Indeed, few cultures have been as aggressive as the Europeans since the end of the Great Bubonic Plague, or White Death, which peaked in the 14th century with more than 100 million people dead. Learned men and women sought ways to explain the meaning of the incredible devastation of people by the pestilence of *Yersinia pestis*. Alongside religious references and conspiracies, there were mythological reimaginations that lent a motivation to the already ingrained attitudes about humanity.

While it is true that the murder of George Floyd in Minneapolis on May 25, 2020, in the midst of the COVID-19 pestilence sparked our desire to write a book about race—the illusory palisade that has surrounded the drive for domination, discrimination, conquest, and justification of the murder of people who were "assigned" places by those who considered themselves of a different order—we are not the first and will not be the last to comment on the enormity of this false construction on world consciousness (Asante, 2015). Yet we see it as our duty to plainly lay out the reasons for the attempts at remaking, remapping, and revising human history to serve the interests of an illusion. As we shall show, there are a plethora of sources indicating that Europeans have felt since the 1400s that there should be those who eat more, use more resources, earn higher wages, be protected by the police, and have more livable conditions than others who are consigned to lower wages, poorer housing, and fewer opportunities because they occupy the "lower races" (Blaut, 1993). This phenomenon is based on the constructed racial ladder that commands so much of the intellectual and social space in the West and, by the projection of the West, in other parts of the world.

Of course, we know by now that the perception of black men by white police in the United States and United Kingdom, as an example, is one dot in the equation of supposed white racial supremacy. How the black man is viewed in contemporary society is most likely a result of the damning use of images, myths, and lies meant to maintain the "ladder" of racial ranking, where whites are at the top and blacks are at the bottom. Tommy J. Curry (2017), in *The Man-Not: Race, Class, Genre and the Dilemmas of Black Manhood*, has provocatively challenged the negation of the black man by showing that in most cases the black man in America is a victim of white racist perceptions created by the racist system of oppression. Although we are most prominently introduced to the immediate problems of black men, it is impossible to separate the problems of black men from those of black women. That is why Nah Dove (1998) wrote *Afrikan Mothers: Bearers of Culture, Makers of Social Change* as an illustration of the resilience of women under the threat of domination by a system that works to undermine the legitimacy of the black woman.

Our work must be seen as being in the tradition of Kendi's (2017) award-winning *Stamped From the Beginning: The Definitive History of Racist Ideas in America*, which established the American empire as being the repository of racist policies and attitudes from the beginning of the nation. However, while we applaud the comprehensive nature of Kendi's research, we are inclined in our work to concentrate on how patriarchy is linked to hierarchy and how both are generators of racial ranking. Furthermore, race as a biological illusion (although discussed in numerous articles and books) remains responsible for racism and the creation of labels such as "Negro," "half-caste," "Indian," "Aryan," "Nordic," "Oriental," and "mulatto." Thus, the reality of race, despite its spurious nature in biology, is dominant in the thinking of white supremacists, neo-Nazis, and racial "purists," who cling to the ranking ladder for fear of tumbling down (Wynter, 2015).

Others have historicized race and racism (Asante, 2009; Banton,1987; Kendi, 2017), but we intend to show how ranked notions of human beings is itself the closed door to social transformation. Furthermore, we find Isabel Wilkerson's *Caste: The Origins of Our Discontents* (2020), a useful and provocative discussion of the structure of inequality. Our intention, however, is to demonstrate what is necessary to eradicate the racial ladder that was created on the basis of physical attributes. Those who profited from the unequal social and economic situations established in law, custom, and practice, and enforced by violence, hardly expected the lowest rung to overturn the entire ladder. Yet it is this superstructure grounded in the illusion of race that condemns societies to distrust. Of course, this idea has been put to destructive ends in societies, pitting one group against another, minimizing histories, distorting records of achievements, and punishing individuals because of fear of competition and so forth. The destruction and deforming of human beings because of a biological illusion of some pure race as different from other humans is not only lunatic, but it also boggles our contemporary imagination that it has been allowed to occupy so much space in the policy decisions of even those individuals who are thought of as progressive, humanists, revolutionaries, and transformers. Thus, we examine the "origins of discontents" but demonstrate the ancient path to overcoming the racial ladder parading as science in the first place.

Our book will also discuss the social and economic symptoms of the illusion because we are most likely as readers to fall into the discourse about race and racism that is often occupied by abuse and brutality; physical violence is the end result of perceptual and conceptual stigma and the actions it leads to. The fact that there have been scores of blacks violently killed by police with little accountability in the past five years means that there has been an acceptable permissible level authorized either legally or customarily by the politicians, some of whom are black, who have bought into the perception of black bodies as being fit for abuse and brutality. Yet it should be clear, as we are certain, that even if police brutality were solved today there will still be "racial" violence against people seen as black because those seen as white have come to accept the ranking ladder that allows any and all types of discrimination, persecution, and killing of blacks.

A society that is pulverized by negativity when it comes to African people will never be able to recover completely from the damage done by the popular cultural promoters of racism. Although our view may not be as dystopian as that found in the works of Ta-Nehisi Coates (*Between the World and Me*, 2015) or the earlier work of Derrick Bell (*Faces at the Bottom of the Well*, 2018), we are quite certain that they both saw what we have seen in the construction of race and its outcome, racism, as projected in policies, programs, promotions, and possibilities. Getting people to forgo what they have been taught in school, convinced of by their racialized parents, and persuaded to believe in by their mosques, churches, temples, and shrines will be a difficult task, but it is one that we must seek to accomplish if we are to become a truly human society.

This book is about humanity. It seeks to dethrone race—not merely to direct the way it can be reconstructed but rather to put a seal on its long, dangerous run in the consciousness of human beings. This will require a straightforward contextualization that will be easily followed. It will mean that we must accept the science that all humans, *Homo sapiens*, originated on the continent of Africa. We know that the people who left the continent of Africa 70,000 years ago were black people since there were no other *Homo sapiens* (Diop, 1974). Science supports a monogenesis thesis, not a polygenesis one. Our book explores how humans descended from the *human* idea to the *race* idea.

However, since Africans and many others have participated in the charade of race, although we did not create it, the time has come for a thorough review, critique, and rejection of the discourse around the illusion of race as having anything to do with how we talk about our humanity. This is precisely what a host of writers, especially from Africa and Asia, have begun to do in their research (Mazama, 2016; Miike, 2014).

The race paradigm both originates with the categorization of humans according to physical traits and leads to the endless classification of humanity according to some racial ladder of superiority and inferiority. That has led to the doctrine of white racial domination, which sits at the entrance to the temple of communication, discourse, international relations, and history.

The invention of race by Europeans was a magical trick played out on the carpet of patriarchy and hierarchy that had existed long before the innovation of race. There was no race consciousness prior to the 15th century; there was differentiation among the populations of the earth based on geography, physical traits, and languages, but differences did not mean social rankings assigned to all humans on earth. Where there were caste and certain ideas of ethnocentrism, they were often local and based on religion.

Race, as a novel explanation for conquest, was the most comprehensive attempt at human division that had ever been created. It was not the only endeavor at division, as there had been barbarians and civilized cultures, light and dark, heathens and chosen ones, enslaved and free, prior to race; yet it was race in its debasement of culture and elevation of ranking based on physical traits that introduced the race illusion and established various palisades around it. The objective was to justify European conquest and subjugation of other "races" as a favored race that was natural and predictable. The assignation of lower status to Africans created a diabolical perception of black people by Europeans and even influenced the way Africans viewed themselves once enslaved and colonized. The same fate happened to many Asians. Hence, prior to the European invention of race, the Greeks held the Nubians and Kemetic people of the Nile Valley among the most advanced people on the earth, to the extent that Herodotus (*Histories*, Book II, 5th century BCE) said that many of the achievements attributed to the Greeks came from the black people of the Nile Valley.

Clearly, it is truly impossible to have a meaningful discussion about racism within the trope of race itself (Jaima, 2019). What is necessary is for humanity to break free of the vise constructed by patriarchies and hierarchies and supported by religious and social ideologies to assign ranking and status to different people. In effect, Afrocentricity has emerged as a new ethic with values based in the traditions of African culture, where human beings were never seen as separate races with status levels controlled by physical characteristics, the basis of the European notions of race. Our discovery of new avenues for discourses around humanity might be radical not because of the collapse of the European Enlightenment paradigm but because of the assertion of the antirace idea of humanity.

Afrocentricity does not make some grand announcement of the end of history, but perhaps it harkens us to the beginning of a new history where *humanity* becomes the only category for *Homo sapiens*. This does not preclude questions of culture, as we shall see, but it complicates the emphasis on biology. As we know, a population living in a particular geographical region for a long time will have propensities for values and experiences that are derived from that background; this we see as culture and not race. Dispensing with racial discourse is just one of the ways by which we attack what everyone now calls the social construction of race. Race can no longer be used as a category for humanity, which means, of course, that we are also attacking the generators of race doctrines, patriarchy, and hierarchy (Dove, 2018).

Using the groundbreaking scholarship of Cheikh Anta Diop, who wrote the important book *The African Origin of Civilization* (1974), we have followed every path toward the common origins of both humanity and civilization on the African continent to demonstrate that culture, while complex, remains a much more neutral term in discussing humans. Ultimately, there are no humans whose DNA did not originate in Africa. Furthermore, the creation of the first nation, Kemet, by the pioneering king Menes is an African achievement. Combining 42 clans into one united government was a monumental event in history that has often been neglected by Western historians. The early sciences and arts, astronomy, medicine, music, politics, biology, geometry, sculpture, agriculture, and anatomy are all credited to the Nile Valley civilizations (Asante, 2019; Diop, 1974).

It was also Diop who wrote the basic outline of the development of early structures of human living on the African continent. In his provocative work *Civilization or Barbarism: An Authentic Anthropology*, Diop (1992) discusses prehistory, race, and history in the context of European researches into the origin of civilization. Diop goes further than most anthropologists had gone at the time to describe the nature of culture and especially cultural identity. His work serves as a guide to many studies that have been done in the African world on human history; we are certainly influenced by Diopian analyses and have brought them forward in our own approach. What we have learned in our own research is that Diop's constructions allow us to severely question patriarchy and hierarchy as engines of ranking and race. This is the challenge of our time because it has added to the danger to African people, who have been ranked by Europeans on the basis of a false construct.

When we have discredited the old patriarchal ways that generate ranking of humans, we will no longer have the so-called racial or social issues around complexion, gender, class, or place of origin that are engendered by speaking of race, class or gender. At such a point, we will only speak of humans of one species, *Homo sapiens*.

Differentiation of humans began in the West with the Graeco-Hebraic-Arabic texts and found inspiration even earlier in the Vedas of India. Consequently, once this road was opened and the adventurous Europeans in the Age of European Exploration journeyed to the Americas, Asia, and Africa, the entire world was soon affected by the way Europe saw human beings. Europe managed to create the hierarchical ranking ladder with doggedly imperialistic notions of European superiority. It has been argued successfully that even the European Crusades between 1096 and 1271 did not establish the concept of race, although Europeans saw and fought with people from Asia and Africa in their campaigns. It appears that the 15th to 19th centuries were the years of systematic development of race as a false concept and racism as an inherent part of the European philosophical framework. Challenging race with humanity will require humility that shows itself as a quest for information, knowledge, and reaction. It is neither arrogant nor disdainful of others. This is not to say that all humans would look the same or be the same in outlook but placing value on biological characteristics particularly and on other attributes that come with humanity will not play a role in our responses to them. Of course, there are some differences that are natural around abilities and capabilities, but these do not inflame the race paradigm.

We write this book as a legitimate strategy to overrun the palisades that have been set up to embolden the racists, to support the race paradigm, and to enshrine the "ranking of races." From the perspective of our discipline, where a common humanity is the principal trope of human civilization, this book makes all arguments against the fortressed paradigm, with tactical moves to bring about social transformation that will further the demise of race and make it easier for righteous activists and progressive politicians to defeat racism in all sectors of human life. The main event, for us, is the emergence of what Dove (2021) refers to as *Maaticity*, a defensive assertion against the false race paradigm in the search for being human. Indeed, Maaticity is a philosophical posture emphasizing the optimum benefits of the ancient idea of *Ma'at*, where truth, righteousness, justice, harmony, order, balance, and reciprocity serve as components of being human beings. It therefore acts as an active theory of ethics, knowledge, and metaphysics. Maaticity is the process of becoming human in a relational sense, where we seek to relate to others, the environment, and the metaphysical world (Karenga, 2003).

The principles of Maaticity form the theoretical framework for becoming. It can only exist because the foundational human culture that arose out of Africa from the beginning of the creation of *Homo sapiens* was based on female and male reciprocity, the ability to create life and culture founded on the development of their harmonious, reciprocal, and just relationship. Without female and male respect, there can be no Ma'at and Maaticity, the route to becoming human. Maatic principles are the foundation on which the judgment of life is made. Based on these principles, we outline how near or far we are from being human beings. Maaticity, the theory of ethics and morality, is ultimately the balance on which actions are weighed. An objective is to name the rights and wrongs from the silenced voices of those not considered human by other cultural terms arising from hierarchy. The voice of the black woman is the least heard in our current global cultural matrix, but she is the key to understanding and applying Maaticity to life.

References and Notes

Asante, M. K. (2009). *Erasing racism. Survival of the American nation.* Prometheus.

Asante, M. K. (2015). *Points of view: Writings on race from diverse perspectives.* Cognella.

Asante, M. K. (2019). *The history of Africa* (3rd ed.). Routledge. https://doi.org/10.4324/9781315168166

Banton, M. (1987). *Racial theories.* Cambridge University Press.

Bell, D. (2018). *Faces at the bottom of the well.* Basic Books.

Blaut, J. M. (1993). *Eight Eurocentric historians.* Guilford Press.

> In this book, Blaut established himself as one of the leading opponents of those who took on white supremacist doctrines claiming some exceptionalism to European culture. What passed as mainstream was merely seen as justification for European historians, eight of them in this book, to assert their arguments for various ideas of superiority. He analyzed the sources and data of the Eurocentric arguments and found them to be self-serving because they were inadequately founded on the principles of our common humanity. His evidence comes from numerous sources and many parts of the world, both before 1492 and afterward, up to 1688. Knowing the geography and history quite well, Blaut lays out the main elements of deceptive reasoning and places them at the foot of the standard arguments for European exceptionalism.

Coates, T.-N. (2015). *Between the world and me.* One World.

Curry, T. (2017). *The Man-Not: Race, Class, Genre, and the Dilemmas of Black Manhood.* Temple University Press.

> The author makes a profoundly well-argued thesis that black masculinity has been maligned since the end of the enslavement of Africans in the United States and critiques the positioning of violence against black males as part of

the promotion of stereotypes reinforced by the media. In a severe reevaluation, Curry argues that some aspects of gender studies have also promoted a view of black masculinity in the same light as white masculinity. Curry's contention is that these studies have imposed negative historical stereotypes and ignored the immense diversity among black boys and men. For us, Curry is useful in seeing the distortions caused not just by the term "race" or the practice of racism but also by the original sin of the creation of the racial ladder by which white people assumed a superior position for white men.

Diop, C. A. (1974). *The African origin of civilization*. Lawrence Hill.

Diop, C. A. (1992). *Civilization or barbarism: An authentic anthropology* (Y.-L. M. Ngemi, Trans.). Chicago Review Press.

Dove, N. (1998). *Afrikan mothers: Bearers of culture, makers of social change*. SUNY Press.

Dove, N. (2018). Race revisited: A cultural construction bearing significant implications. *International Journal of African Renaissance Studies, 13*(2), 129–143. https://doi.org/10.1080/18186874.2018.1538703

Dove, N. (2021, July 11). *Interpreting Maat for contemporary society* [Letter to Molefi Kete Asante].

Karenga, M. (2003). *Maat: The moral ideal in Ancient Egypt*. Routledge. https://doi.org/10.4324/9780203502686

Kendi, I. X. (2017). *Stamped from the beginning: The definitive history of racist ideas in America*. Bold Type Press.

Kendi, I. X. (2019). *How to be an antiracist*. One World.

Mazama, A. (2016). Afrocentricity and the critical question of African agency. In A. Akomolafe, M. K. Asante, & A. Nwoye (Eds.), *We will tell our own story!* (pp. 52–74). Universal Write.

Miike, Y. (2014). The Asiacentric turn in Asian communication studies: Shifting paradigms and changing perspectives. In M. K. Asante, Y. Miike, & J. Yin (Eds.), *The global intercultural communication reader* (2nd ed., pp. 111–133). Routledge.

Wilkerson, I. (2020). *Caste: The origins of our discontents*. Random House.

> Brilliantly written by a Pulitzer Prize–winning author, this book traces the notions of race and caste to similar origins. In some ways, the book anticipates our work, which seeks to establish an actionable way of understanding and destroying the instruments that maintain inequalities and brutalities.

Wynter, S. (2015). *No humans involved* (On the Blackness of BlackNUSS). Publication Studio Hudson.

CHAPTER 1

Patriarchy: The Origin of Hierarchy and Race

In the middle of winter on January 6, 2021, during the most devastating period of the COVID-19 plague, thousands of followers of President Donald Trump rampaged through the U.S. Capitol building, raffling through documents and storming every room they could find in search of members of Congress with the intent to stop the certifying of the electoral college's votes in order to insert Trump as the winner of the 2020 presidential election (Claire, 2021). The insurrectionists claimed in a tragic rage that Joe Biden had stolen the election from Trump, which was untrue, although at the core of their agitative spirit was a sense of the breaking down of white hegemony in a multicultural, pluralistic, and dynamic nation (Parker et al., 2019). Stuck in the past glories of killing black women, men, and children with impunity, covered with the bloodied blanket of the Confederate history around their shoulders, they shouted that they were "taking back their country," and while roaming through the Capitol building looking for Vice President Mike Pence and Speaker Nancy Pelosi, they shouted, "Where are they?" Fortunately for the second and third persons in line to run the country and other congresspeople and senators, they had been swiftly taken to a safe area. Nevertheless, the mob attacked the police and, in its madness, kept beating a white man, who screamed, "You are treating me like I am a black person!" Assaulting a police officer named Dunn, who was defending the Capitol building, a female Trump supporter yelled to the crowd that "this nigger voted for Biden!"

There was a sense that the mob felt white privilege, while its members had seen the election as the loss of white privilege, as it attacked the Capitol. The thugs wanted a white society, an anti-Jewish, anti-African, and anti-Arab nation, despite the demographic transformations that had happened in the nation since the end of the 20th century. Some African American writers had anticipated this reaction or had warned against relaxing while neo-Nazis and white supremacists marched throughout the nation during the Trump presidency displaying their Nazi and Confederacy symbols and flags to announce their anger at their loss of hegemony in many circles (Asante, 2018). During the 2020 presidential election, the majority of white voters chose Trump, while other whites, blacks, Asian Americans, Latin Americans, and Native Americans chose Biden. White supremacists were told by the demagogue Trump that he had won the election, and they figured that there was no way the white majority could have lost the election (Asante, 2018). In effect, the white insurrectionists played out the race episteme to its conclusion—violence.

Our intent is to question the white supremacist epistemes that use race as a determinant for defining the status of the humanity of African women, men, and children. Other writers have challenged this abiding dilemma where the construction of race has been used as a plow to uncover or to bury power relationships between people from time to time (Feagin, 2006). In the face of race, a prevailing and seemingly unanswerable question emerges as to what Africa has got to do with anything progressive and futuristic concerning humanity.

We advocate the ancient principles of harmony, order, justice, truth, righteousness, reciprocity, and balance as we introduce humanity as a way around discourses on race and hierarchy (Karenga, 2006). Maulana Karenga's *Maat: The Moral Ideal in Ancient Egypt* (2006) is the most comprehensive and magisterial treatment of the role of ethics in becoming human. Early African cultures considered becoming human a process like the transformation of a scarab beetle, often referred to as a dung beetle because it lays its egg in a ball of dung that it rolls across the ground. Finally, after metamorphosis from larva to adult, the egg in the ball of dung reaches a new stage.

This is precisely the reason why they called the beetle *Khepera*, which means "to become," or transformation. *Khepera* was used as an amulet to reflect transformation, immortality, and protection in Ancient Africa. Our point is that the abandonment of the illusion of race allows us to seek Ma'at and thus the real meaning of humanity based on the ancient principles. Like someone who has lost her way, we seek to trace our path back to the origin and begin the process of transformation omitting, as much as possible, the bog of race.

Afrocentric theory has created, inter alia, *sebayet* ("wisdom") outside Eurocentric and Arabo-centric epistemes, placing Africa and African women, men, and children at the center of human reality. This condition can be very frightening and even threatening for people of African descent trained in epistemes that have created negative phantasmagorial ideas about Africa and her people that have over time justified false beliefs about Africa and African people (Curry, 2017). As an academic, one finds oneself consumed by trying to prove one's own humanity and that of other black/African women, men, and children. However, the more one acquiesces to these academic falsehoods, the easier it becomes to progress through the Pan-European Academy. That is why the Afrocentric episteme brings fear of believing that Africa is the opposite of the way it has been portrayed for centuries. This falsehood about Africa is a violation against the human code of ethics or the human norm from an Afrocentric cultural perspective. In reality, Africology has an important role in questioning the authority of non-African epistemes that use race, based on the melanin content of the skin, as a determinant for defining the status of the humanity of African women, men, and children.

The ongoing Afrocentric work has become all the more relevant in this special moment that has arisen around the blatant public murder of George Floyd. In the main, we, the African and Diaspora people of the world, are aware of the brutality meted out against black women, men, and children for countless centuries (Aptheker, 1951/1975). Unlike all the other times, Floyd's murder was caught on video—not just a photo but a moving image of a living man dying, with a clearly arrogant white man mounted on him with his knee on Floyd's neck, as if his victim were a safari trophy, while enjoying the sensation of feeling Floyd's life slowly ebb away in horror and pain. Derek Chauvin felt safe in the knowledge that the construct of race, with its inherent demonization and debasement of black women, men, and children; the racist global world system of governance; and his president would support him and he would be exonerated by "the law" in the same way as those who came before. Unsurprisingly, we were notified on *BBC News Online* on October 7, 2020, that Chauvin was released on $1 million bail.

Black Lives Matter led in rousing those disgusted and appalled by the event, which raised global dissent as people across the world of all races identified and criticized their own racist social systems. In light of this special moment, there has been a growing awareness that the race theory and paradigm can no longer explain the continuous hatred meted out to black people on account of their being black, or the desire for being white, the epitome of humanity. If we are seriously supposed to believe in progress and evolution, how come we are essentially at the same place in terms of the value of black lives after all these years of protest against a backlog of horror concerning the enslavement and maltreatment of African women,

men, and children for 500 years in the Americas and at least 2,000 years under Hebraic/Islamic/Christian rule?

It is necessary to bring clarity and understanding to the construction and invention of race as a human hierarchy in its objective to rationalize privilege based on the melanin content of the skin. As a result of the need for race inventors to place black/African women, men, and children at the base of this hierarchy, the recognition of this falsehood has been led by those most despised by it. The spearhead to this movement is led by mothers and fathers who ask, "How can I raise my babies to understand their beauty and humanity in a world that despises us"?

The difference in the account of how and why this construction took place is led by Afrocentric theory, the foundation of the discipline of Africology—the study of Africa and all phenomena pertaining to Africa. Afrocentric theory provides a grounded analytical stance on the ideas, researched studies, and works that have been developed over time that speak to whether or not they are founded on the love of Africa and her people. Afrocentric theory asks these questions:

> What is the intention of the work?
> Does the work exhibit the potential for enlightenment and development?
> Do the ideas intend to improve the lives of women, men, and children of African descent, in particular the most "melaninated" at the base of the hierarchy of race?

It is understood that the use of varying anti-African epistemes has often clouded the judgment of African thinkers, ideologists, writers, and academics, possibly leading to the support of enemies of Africa and the betrayal of Africa in all forms, from the religious to the political. Africology, the discipline that employs Afrocentricity in its analysis, looks to indigenous knowledge of Africa before its conquest for locating and examining the historical processes that led us to this point. Africology is a discipline grounded in nearly 2,000 years of ancestral voices calling for restorative justice regarding the untold endless struggles, unspeakable cruelty, genocide, abuse, dehumanization, enslavement, murder, mistreatment, debasement, and demonization of African people, in particular the blackest, that is, the most melaninated humanity.

The theory and concept of race will be examined with a discerning eye that will override the concepts of race that are called by other names and precede the current usage. This will bring to light some of the hidden and disguised forms of racism. Every human hierarchy that uses color—the melanin content in the skin—to designate a status to people, where the blackest people are at the bottom, will be considered racist, whether the label used is caste, ethnicity, class, gender, or some other term. To these labels, titles, and definitions, we add Latinx, Hispanics, and so on.

The cultural construction of race challenges the theorizing of race as a social construct. There is undeniably a social construction of race. We are social beings, but culture is what connects us to the way we socialize or even plan the type of society that we wish to develop. Culture is what influences humans to build societies in different ways. There are three important contemporary academic disciplines that relate specifically to understanding what it is to be human. Essentially, and simply put, (1) sociology is the study of humanity and behaviors, including the study of societies; (2) psychology is the study of human behavior and the workings of the mind, and their interaction with societies; and (3) anthropology is the study of humanity relating to culture and its impact on human behavior, human biology, and societies. These three major disciplines can be separated into different fields of interest:

- Anthropological studies can focus on the influences of linguistic, physical, biological, and social life.
- Sociology focuses on social development, with a focus on institutional development; thus, one may study individual institutions like

family, education, politics, health, sports, entertainment, economies, spiritual systems, and so on.
- Psychology separates the workings of the mind in clinical psychology, using a more scientific approach to mental health care, as opposed to social psychology, which recognizes the impact of society on the behaviors and thoughts of humans, thus needing an understanding of both social and cultural knowledge to make sense of what it is to be human.

What tends to happen is that Eurocentric academic disciplines are disconnected from each other, so that studies and research are undertaken without straying into other disciplines, the majority of which have a stated interest in humanity in common, like philosophical thought and history. This separatism is common to most Eurocentric disciplines. Moreover, there is a similarity in a historical and theoretical sense in that the modern versions of sociology, psychology, and anthropology were codified in the 19th century.

We say "modern" because we believe that academic training and ideas of this nature go back several thousand years before Rome and Greece to Africa, in the sense that humans have been studying humanity with a more holistic awareness and approach to these studies, some of which has been written, symbolized, and memorialized, manifesting in the behaviors, values, and beliefs of more ancient societies (Asante, 1987; Bernal, 2006; Diop, 1974; Hilliard, 1998; James, 1989; Rashidi, 2017; Van Sertima, 1976; Williams, 1992).

The end of the 18th and the beginning of the 19th century, during the development of these disciplines, augured the continuation of the horrific experience for African women, men, and children captured, enslaved, and mercilessly debased and demonized by Arabs and Europeans alike, attested to by their religious beliefs, behaviors, and writings. This inhuman behavior—noting that "inhuman" is generally understood as barbarous, without compassion, cruel, and savage—defined and continues to define the treatment of people of African descent. The profits from the "black gold" (a term coined by Karl Marx), underpinned by the acquisition of untold wealth, created the ability to build cities across the world, financed the so-called Industrial Revolution, and furnished academic studies in Europe (Dove, 1995). Creating and substantiating the pseudoscientific idea that human development is linked to human evolution rationalized the continuing brutish enslavement of African women, men, and children. Thus, over time, Europeans, especially those whose families directly benefited from this holocaust and those whose families benefited indirectly, of all classes, sexes, genders, and castes across the world have learned to support this unconscionable behavior, which some of us, even as African/black women, men, and children, have also come to believe is natural to humanity.

These racist beliefs were supported, justified, theorized, and fed to the academic world in the guise of unbiased and objective beliefs, in that academics thought that their research could or should be unemotional, grounded in truth, and neutral in fields such as history, biology, sociology, anthropology, psychology, and education (Dove, 1995).

Afrocentric theory demands a discourse that privileges African reality from the perspective of humanity and civilization. Such investigation admits to its particular standpoint on reality since *Homo sapiens* arose in Africa and all basic structures of civilization, from naming to surviving, also started in Africa. In this way, our work is considered agency based in the sense that we propose that the African voice must be asserted and heard in all issues related to African reality. We have often recognized and discerned a European bias in academic works claimed to be objective and neutral. In this light, our work will possibly appear as a polemic (from the Greek word *polemikos*), that is, a contentious narrative that supports, in our case, a specific African perspective that challenges anti-African/black theories. To bring clarity to the limitations of race as a social construct idea, this work will view race as a cultural construction based on belief in a human hierarchy. The concept of culture and its significance to human development recognizes the social construction of race and other concepts that have dominated our thinking in the discourse around patriarchy and hierarchy. Consider the often inadequate conversation around black women and gender issues.

Dark-skinned women and men left Africa around 70,000 years ago after spending nearly two thirds of *Homo sapiens*' time on the continent developing African matriarchal beliefs, taking Maatic principles, ancestral remembrances, families, and skills with them across the world. We note at this point that Inzalo Y'Langa in South Africa, the massive stone complex, was already in existence prior to these early migrations, as were bone tools dating 90,000 years ago found in the Congo (Yellen et al., 1995). We also know more recently that the Lebombo bone, 35,000 years old, found in South Africa, depicting the movements of the moon in relation to women's periods, and the similar instrument of counting found among the Ishango people of Congo, which goes back to 28,000 years ago, represent creations of humans on the African continent. One may mistakenly consider that the use of bone for tools and astronomy is a sign of simple construction, yet bone lasts as evidence that humans were creative, as we are today. Either women or men invented these items; we do not know which. From the vantage point of evolutionists, race believers, and patriarchs, who believe in the superiority of white women and men, the epitome of humanity in the march toward civilization, to believe that these African women and men, supposedly still beasts, not fully human, left Africa with principles of higher learning is outside their stultified comprehension, even for some who read this book. For religious believers in black women's and men's inferiority, our perspective is blasphemous, so much so that it cannot be tolerated. To believe in the humanity of African women, men, and children is to challenge all that we have been taught through investigation, study, and research, carried out with tainted and bloodied tools of analysis, sanctified holy, spiritual, and unquestionable in the eyes and mind, epistemically, of those who subscribe to our inhumanness. Even the notion of African women as reciprocal partners to African men is considered nonsense, although some would say like J. J. Bachofen, Lewis Henry Morgan, and Frederick Engels that this egalitarian relationship is a lower stage in human development (Diop, 1989). What does this mean when there is evidence of this continuing relationship existing in deep structure in the African world even during enslavement and colonization? The race–patriarchy paradigm of evolution and progress views female–male reciprocity as evidence of African inferiority rather than evidence of a civilizing practice that espouses the values of Ma'at, toward which humanity seeks to go. Sometimes this reciprocity is hidden, sometimes evident, depending on the cultural intrusion and imposition of an anti-African, anti-black image of women, men, and children on our minds, whether institutionally, spiritually, or theoretically. Some will consider the notion of patriarchy to be flawed in addressing the real power of the African woman, and of no value in understanding African reality. However, our position is that we acknowledge patriarchy as fundamental to the debasement of women, and we go further to suggest that patriarchy is the cultural root of the construction of race, formed from the patriarchal bond, a covenant fashioned by women and men to "hierarch-ize" themselves above all phenotypes, nature, the cosmos, the divinities, and so on, thereby tolerating and concealing the first injustice, domination, with the compensation of being greater than all others, and empowering one another in the quest to justify the sacredness of that covenant. In hierarchy, there is always something or someone beneath who can be controlled, dominated, disrespected, abused, and so on. We see examples in the categories of lumpen proletarian, untouchables, underclass, weeds, mongrels, and so on. We see hierarchy imposed not only in the racialization of humanity but also in theories that rely on concepts of class, gender, sex, and ethnicity to explain human oppressions. From our perspective, race and patriarchy cannot be separated from each other or these cultural and social structures, which would not exist without them.

In terms of gender, Chandler (1999) explains that his use of "feminine" and "masculine" does not correspond one-to-one with the terms "woman" and "man" since by the law of polarity feminine and masculine are simply the two shades of gender. By the law of gender, all things are feminine *and* masculine; it follows that all people embody all shades of gender. If gender is conceptualized on a scale, the poles of which are pure femaleness and maleness, then we see how we have come to label people female or male. Those who are psychologically and physically closer to the female pole are called women, and those closer to the male pole are called men. Though many of us choose to view this scale as fixed or steadfast, our present social, cultural, as well as psychological circumstances dictate a broader reality, informing us of the potentiality of more than two types of sexes. It is gender, operating within the parameters of polarity, that makes this a possibility. Gender, apart from its modern association with sex, is the process of begetting, generating, creating, and producing on all planes of creation. "Positive" and "negative" when applied to gender are never antagonistic to each other but work mutually in continuous harmony. One is dependent on the other in the process of being and becoming; they are complements, not opposites.

Following this logic, with the awareness that European cultural beliefs focus on gender as sexual, the Ibo and Yoruba languages challenge European ideas on what constitutes women and men (Amadiume, 1987a, 1992; Oyěwùmí, 1997). The imposition of European languages on defining African female/male realities invokes rigid ideas of gender as sexualized. We note that enforcing a language is a necessary part of cultural domination in that it subscribes to the institutional impositions that are a critical part of nation-states developed all over Africa that are anti-African, against black women, men, and children, and subscribe to the institutional cultural needs of the oppressor. In the case of European and Arab beliefs imposed across Africa, the domination of women, the color-coded ideas of superiority and inferiority, and ethnic and religious separations are basic. Essentially, this condition is to prevent African women and men from working together toward liberation; in reality, all liberation has taken place through the concerted efforts of women and men, although these realities have been conveniently hidden. European and Arabic nation-states in Africa have been successful in their objectives to separate African people and normalize this disconnection, owing to the heinous crimes of abuse, violence, and genocide committed during their construction. In this way, disconnection and dislocation serve to support the academic propaganda that claims that Africa is so different culturally, historically, linguistically, spiritually, and psychologically, that there is no similitude. This falsehood begs the question regarding the cultural unity of the conquerors, who clearly discerned cultural unity among their victims, as evidenced in their methods of domination. We believe that prior to conquest, African people had similar values and beliefs. In relation to women and men, gendered roles were very likely not rigid, as we have claimed, and this would be logical from our viewpoint regarding female–male reciprocity. We can see this in everyday lives across the continent as well as among the African diaspora, and we believe that continuing research will over time codify this reality into academic form. Ifi Amadiume (1987a, 1992), who dedicated her 1987 book *African Matriarchal Foundations: The Igbo Case* to Cheikh Anta Diop (1923–1986), the Senegalese multigenius, linguist, scientist, Egyptologist, educationist, sociologist, and anthropologist, exposes how the rigidity of sexualized genders in Europe has had an impact on how research is constructed in Africa relating to the roles of women, who like men can shift into differing gendered roles to uphold families and institutions from the spiritual to the economic. Thus, the idea of African women as powerful leaders, as in the case of the priestesses, and other labeled queens in Kemet, such as Peraat Neith-Hotep, who ruled around 3080 BCE (much earlier if one accepts the Manetho date, which would be 5581 BCE), appears earlier than anywhere else in the world (Walker, 2006). Neith-Hotep, whose name Neith means "the deity of warfare is pleased," is called the Consort of the Two Ladies, Nekhbet ("vulture") and Wadjet ("snake"). Therefore, this fact supports the idea that prior to the conquest of the land by patriarchs, whether the Hyskos, Assyrians, Persians, Greeks, Romans, Turks, and Arabs in Kemet and later the Portuguese, Spanish, British, French, Germans, Swedish, Dutch, Belgians, Norwegians, and Arabs across Africa, women held key leadership positions in the physical realm as well as the spiritual realm. European, Indo-Aryan, Hebraic, and Arabic gendered roles have created immeasurable harm to Africa. We include Indo-Aryan and Hebraic beliefs as their teachings while not centered in Africa have inspired European and Arabic religiosity and concretized their beliefs in patriarchy and race. African women are marginalized as biologically inferior on the grounds of race and sex, and their roles in the spiritual realm have also been demonized and forbidden. Women's roles in institutional development have been curtailed as a fundamental feature of cultural domination. Patriarchy, marginality, hatred, if you will, is perhaps nowhere more pronounced than in the Indo-Aryan Brahmin religion in South Asia, where, according to the Laws of Manu (Olivelle, 2005) in consideration of women, particularly black women, the following beliefs hold (Chandler, 1999):

1. The mind of woman brooks no discipline, for her intellect has little weight.
2. To kill women and Sudras (blacks) one need not worry, for it is not a sin.
3. A mother who remarries, a beautiful wife, and a disobedient son are enemies and may be left with no sin.

4. We should always act with caution with fire, water, women, and snakes, for they may, if an occasion presents itself, at once put you to death.
5. One single object (a woman) appears in three different ways: To the man who practices austerities, she appears as a corpse; to the sensual man, she appears as a woman; and to dogs, she is a lump of flesh.
6. Untruthfulness, rashness, guile, stupidity, avarice, uncleanness, and cruelty are woman's seven natural faults.
7. Women have hunger twofold, shame fourfold, inconsideration sixfold, and lust eightfold more than men.

Hierarchical Thinking

A Brahmana's strength is in his learning, a king's strength is in his army, a Vaishya's strength is in his wealth and a Sudra's strength is in his attitude of service. (Olivelle, 2005, Manu 2:16)

A Brahmana who is only a brahman by descent i.e., one who has neither studied nor performed any other act required by the Vedas may, at the king's pleasure, interpret the law to him i.e., act as the judge, but never a Sudra, however learned he may be. (Olivelle, 2005, Manu 4:99).

The Sudra was created by the self-created one solely to do slave labor for the Brahmin. Even when he is released by his master, a Sudra is not freed from his slave status for that is innate in him; and who can remove it from him? (Olivelle, 2005, Manu 8:413,414).

Candalas and Svepacas (Dalits), however, must live outside the village. . . . Their property consists of dogs and donkeys, their garments are the clothes of the dead, they eat in broken vessels, their ornaments are of iron. . . . A man who follows the Law should never seek any dealing with them. . . . They depend on others for food and it should be given in a broken vessel. They must not go about in villages and towns at night; they may go around during the day to perform some tasks at the command of the king, wearing distinguishing marks. They should carry away the corpses of those without relatives. . . . They should always execute those condemned to death. (Olivelle, 2005, Manu 10:51–56)

It is no wonder Dr. Babasaheb Ambedkar declared that the Manu Smriti (Laws of Manu) was a symbol of injustice. In 1927, he led the burning of the Laws of Manu, and in 1956, he persuaded many Mahar people to leave the Hindu religion. The most extensive form of inequality based on birth exists in the doctrine of Manu, whether it is one's profession, gender, or economic or social status.

African Matriarchy

In African matriarchy, the reality is that women and men take on the roles that they are equipped to do and there is freedom to do what is necessary physically, mentally, and spiritually that can be institutionalized in the best way for societies to develop. Certainly, mothers and fathers are well equipped to notice skills among the children, and their sex need not preclude them from employing their skills. Most important, there is respect for those who carry out the roles, and none of the roles is considered hierarchical in relation to another. For example, we know that because of the nature of conquest, where some people are deemed less than others in nation-states even though they may have lived on ancestral lands for centuries, those who control political and economic power can often deny others access to resources. Yet it is possible to see how gendered roles can be exploited. If a young boy goes to the river to carry water in a bucket on his head along with the girls in rural areas where water is scarce and one must travel some considerable distance to get it, or even go to the village pump, the young boy is not ridiculed, because he must do this for his family to survive. If the family rear cattle and there are no boys to travel with the cattle, a girl will take on the role. She is respected, not reviled. To apply European class and gender hierarchies to African life is problematic and has proved to be destructive in the areas of identifying and imposing them as so-called advancements in particular. Oyèrónkẹ́ Oyěwùmí's ideas regarding the Yoruba language in reference to the roles of women and men raises the idea that in a European notion of gender, there is a construction of women and men that is not true to how masculine and feminine roles are perceived culturally among the Yoruba people. For instance, one would speak of scientists or farmers before one would speak of women or men as both can exist within these roles as a norm. Oyěwùmí notes that from a European theoretical perspective, when studying historical events, the researcher may consider those in leadership positions to be men whereas they may be women. Both women and men may hold the same or similar names and rankings. For Oyěwùmí, age has much more of a bearing in terms of responsibilities and roles. One may speak of mothers who are women; however, as we have noted earlier, in some African societies, a man may be a mother, and indeed the title of mother is considered a high honor. As Eleni Tedla (1995) taught us in *Sankofa: African Thought and Education*, it is necessary to allow Africans to speak their truths about the nature of education and socialization. Importantly, while men may be mothers, women may also not be mothers in the literal sense, but for both, it is the responsibility and compassion that women or men hold that signify their status.

Much later, and in contradiction to these original principles, the backbone of a spiritual moral order, patriarchy evolved. We have said that the first injustice was the domination, repression, and eventual downfall of women; this was the source of the construction of the hierarchy of humanity, race, and white supremacy. Indeed, the domination of women enabled men, and ultimately women, to develop behaviors in opposition and thus antithetical to their original ancestral beliefs. This situation we may view as current.

Much as Carter G. Woodson claimed as far back as 1933 in *The Miseducation of the Negro*, even African academics, both women and men, continue to employ European and Indo-Aryan/Arabo-Hebraic academic teachings, epistemes, and disciplines grounded in the race paradigm to develop liberationist theories. Black feminism, in the main theoretically grounded in patriarchal feminist theory, seeks to find respect in race concepts from cultural groups that have historically, theoretically, spiritually, and in reality been responsible for the murder, debasement, demonization, and undermining of black/African womanhood and mothering (Dove, 1998). An African mother, in whatever cultural context, status, and historical era, of necessity questions the authenticity of any society in which her children will be born. She is the bearer of those who betrayed her, murdered her, denied and demonized her ancestral spiritual links, and committed heinous crimes against her personhood. She has given birth to disenfranchised people throughout the world and enslaved girls and boys to enrich her Semitic/Arabic and white European mistresses and masters, future prisoners enslaved to create profit for Western and Westernizing legal systems, and the Sudras and Dalits of Brahmanism to carry out horrendous servile functions. Countless women and men (her children) are thinkers, writers, healers, priestesses, priests, mathematicians, builders, scientists, farmers, traders, artisans, doctors, warriors, and freedom fighters. She is also the mother of unknown women and men who have fought to change societal conditions in order to reveal the illogical nature of the racial hierarchy (a falsehood) or contest it through action.

Audre Lorde (2018) employed racist European feminist theory, the belief that all women have always been dominated and controlled by all men, to analyze her own situation as a black, lesbian feminist. Theoretically and within this paradigm, she taught us to be extremely careful in defining a liberationist agenda for black women. She asks, "What does it mean when the tools of racist patriarchy are used to examine the fruits of that same patriarchy? It means that only the most narrow perimeters of change are possible and allowable" (p. 17). Lorde's view of "difference" is related to "other," a term borrowed by the white feminist Simone de Beauvoir (2011) from Emmanuel Levinas (1987) in *Time and the Other*, in reference to defining the white woman in relation to the white man as a way of understanding the imposed hierarchy of women's inferiority. Beauvoir (2011) questions whether there is such a thing as a woman. "What is a woman?" she asks (p. 3). She implies that women have been constructed. We may relate this condition of wondering to the supposed first man, Adam, in the Hebraic creation story, who creates the first woman, Eve, from a bone in his rib cage (Genesis 2:21–22). Lorde (2018) relates this term "other" primarily to her degraded human status within the European episteme, which has been responsible for the demonization of African humanity, from Noah's son Ham, who committed the sin of castration on his father, which would justify and ensure the enslavement and debasement of African men and women, including George Floyd, Breonna Taylor, and many more on into an eternal future, on the grounds of their being black. Lorde, an African mother, who bore a child to a white man, sought a world in which all can flourish. She believed that

> it is learning about how to take our differences and make them strengths. For the master's tools will never dismantle the master's house. They may allow us temporarily to beat him at his own game, but they will never allow us to bring about genuine change. (p. 19)

We do not believe the white feminist theory that men have dominated women from the beginning of time. Theoretically for us, we include the mistress and her role as mother, sister, auntie, or grandmother both in the construction of racist beliefs and as a beneficiary of the doctrine of white supremacy.

It has been proven that the African woman is the mother of humanity. We recognize her reciprocal relationship with the African man; thus, we must rethink the contrived "evidence" of her inferiority and subservience to man. Indeed, these anti-African/black women religious beliefs are the bedrock for demonizing the status of women. In the Bible, the woman is said to have committed the first sin in the Garden of Eden; in the Indo-Aryan Brahmin religion, she is debased in her status as a Dalit or Sudra; and the blackest African women, enslaved by today's Islamic men and women in the Sudan, are often called "Zanj," a derogatory name very likely linked to the idea of their insolence in rising up against their barbaric enslavement in the salt fields of Iraq in the 9th century, a reality that resides deep in the cultural memory of their enslavers. In the Sudan, better known as "land of slaves" by the Arabs, the blackest Sudanese women—descendants of the Kushite women, who gave birth to the people of Kemet, so highly respected for its achievements, who bravely fought the Romans to maintain their Kushite lands—are today taken to different parts of the Arab world and Europe as enslaved women. Other Arabized African countries like Mauritania, Algeria, and Libya are guilty of the continuing enslavement of African women, men, and children. This diabolical herstorical treatment is hidden and supported by the academically held theories that are founded on the belief in the inferiority of African humanity as well as the massive profits accumulated from the exploitation of the bodies of black women, men, and children. Ironically, instead of looking to Africa for the cultural connection to our lost ancestors so brutally treated, some of whom resided in the United States as descendants enslaved and brought here, some of us as academicians, African women and men, claim along with Europeans and Arabs that Africology has a romanticized theory of Africa, that her greatness was never true, and furthermore that her debasement and demonization are not relevant to today's African/black women and men. The idea of separation of African people into different nation-states, languages, religions, classes, genders, and sex enables different histories and herstories to be contrived to suit the needs of the conquerors so that we remain purposefully ignorant of who we are. And yet, interestingly, the glorification of European and Semitic conquests across Africa that were entirely demonic and murderous, so much so that those who did not acquiesce to domination were labeled beasts and murdered and some of those who became Arabized or Europeanized lived, is viewed romantically, and their actions are seen as necessarily righteous religiously and justified in the name of progress and becoming civilized.

European/white women have created studies of women as if women are all the same in their domination by men, thereby ignoring their culturally historical involvement in the conquest and demonization of African women, men, and children across the world and in the taking of their lands, wealth of knowledge, energies, and resources from rivers, seas, minerals, gold, oil, diamonds, emeralds, rubies, silver, tanzanite, coltan, petrol, foods, agriculture, forests, and so on. European women have often taken the lead in teaching "other" women that those women have been denied their humanity by men from the beginning of time, thereby denying their responsibility for and involvement with cultural domination and imperialism through enslavement and colonization. We reiterate that all European and Indo-Aryan/Arabo-Hebraic academic disciplines are grounded in anti-black/African beliefs, with the exception of the discipline of Africology. Thus, women using these racist epistemes that deny the humanity of black women find difficulty in reconstructing herstories that love African women and men. Academic disciplines grounded in these epistemes teach black women to critique black men as patriarchs from the beginning of humanity. In this way, the power and agency of African women as black women are denied as a cultural and social reality, and African women remain at the foot of the hierarchy of humanity as they are both black and women. In the effort to separate women from men and nurture a viable relationship among women, African women are asked to develop a belief that European women who have profited from controlling the wealth of black women within the annals of white supremacy are better able to advise, lead, and guide women toward their liberation from male domination. The evolutionist idea claims their leadership as natural. Challenging these ideas, Clenora Hudson-Weems (2019) has made it clear that

> Africana Womanism—rather than feminism, Black feminism, African feminism, or Womanism—is a conceivable alternative for the Africana woman in her collective struggle with the entire community, it enhances future possibilities for the dignity of Africana people and the humanity of all. In short, the reclamation of Africana women via identifying our own collective struggle and acting upon it is a key step toward human harmony and survival. (p. 19)

A fear of patriarchal women is that if African matriarchal women were ever empowered to lead, then they would be, in the Darwinian sense of evolution and progress, at a lower or more primitive stage of development on the route toward civilization from barbarism as both African and women. Within the deep recesses of cultural memory, the African woman is believed to be underequipped to lead. Of course, to go farther back into that memory to a time prior to the doctrines of white and Semitic supremacy would require the relocation of humanity back to its birthplace. The Africologist understands that dislocation from Africa is the key to reviling ancestral appreciation and the continuing loss of memory.

Amadiume (1987a, 1992) famously critiqued the ways European men have led in the development of anthropological research and European women in the study of African women, using anti-African theory to analyze culturally African beliefs. From our Afrocentric vantage point, prior to enslavement, we believe that African women held important positions of responsibility in every institutional domain, such as family, health care, education, economics, entertainment, spirituality, art, architecture, science, manufacturing, agriculture, invention, and so on. She goes on to explain that male and female social roles may interchange, unlike the European gender roles, which are rigidly associated with sex. There is a biological gender distinction for any species among the Ibo people, which is reflected in language. *Oke* is "male" and *nyi* is "female," but in referring to "man," he is *nwoke*, and "woman" is *nwanyi*. The word for "child" is *nwa*, and *oke* and *nyi* are used to distinguish the child's gender. However, no confirmation is made to define whether the person is a *she* or *he*. The Igbo language has genderless words, normalizing the idea that either sex may carry out the same roles. Thus, gender and biological sex are separated. Accepted roles for women and men, if necessary, will be filled by the opposite sex carrying out the same role. Such roles are exemplified in *Male Daughters, Female Husbands: Gender and Sex in an African Society* (Amadiume, 1987b).

We can use Oyěwùmí's ideas with regard to Kemet in that the study of female and male roles has been largely carried out by racist patriarchal men and women, who have presumed the roles that white/European women, not African women, have played to be peripheral, whereas those deemed priests may well have been priestesses who as educators existed in every realm of institutional development. Moreover, as Oyěwùmí has shown, age has a powerful influence on gender roles; we may see this in the role of Queen Tye and her grandson Tutankhamun. We may go back as far as 90,000 years to the tools of women and men in the Congo (Yellen et al., 1995); in South Africa, we have the Inzalo Y'Langa, built 100,000 years ago, evidence of stone architecture with a focus on round buildings, not dissimilar to the later stone architecture of the nearby great Zimbabwe, said to have been constructed in 1100 CE. We are saying that race and patriarchy are not African concepts and that African women and men have been creating institutions for thousands of years, but we can only understand this by riding on top of the surf of culture, which will bring us to the proper human shore about gender and race.

Without the inclusion of culture in our analysis, there is a tendency, because of Eurocentric epistemes, to view the construction and practice of race as an autonomous entity, appearing to be a natural phenomenon that all people practiced at one time or other. In this way, there is a justification for its existence, as if it is a social norm or a stage of human development that may remain or disappear. Thus, policies regarding the importance of antiracist training, behaviors, and so on are unable to get to the root of its existence but merely put a bandage on a suppurating disease. There appears to be no origin or blame as it appears that we have all practiced the racialization of humanity; thus, heinous crimes continue to take place openly, as in the case of George Floyd and Breonna Taylor and millions of other black women, men, and children across the Americas and the world. This acceptance feeds into the dulling of any semblance of truth, justice, and righteousness, beyond the rhetoric. The truth is that not all cultures, societies, and therefore social structures are racist.

Culture will be used as the key to understand its powerful influence on human institutional development. While culture is essentially an anthropological idea, anthropologists along with explorers, biologists, linguists, historians, philosophers, physicians, theologians, writers, scientists, mathematicians, explorers, and others have been guilty of defining culture within a racialized hierarchy, at least since the 1700s, beginning with Carl Linnaeus (1707–1778), who described the African person as the *Afer* or *Africanus*: black, phlegmatic, relaxed; frizzled hair; silky skin, flat nose, tumid lips; women without shame; mammary glands giving milk abundantly; crafty, sly, lazy, cunning, lustful, careless; anointing himself with grease; and governed by caprice (Gould, 1981).

In the main, anthropologists have justified racist ideas about Africa and/or black people and used their focus on culture to classify values and beliefs, using the theory of race to support their concept of culture. Culture in this light has been used as a comparative method of defining humanity, supporting race-based evolutionist theories that denote African inferiority, seemingly substantiated in the beliefs, values, and behaviors of so-called primitives.

Diop changed this Eurocentric course of thinking by de-racializing and redefining the concept of culture and centering Africa as the cradle of humanity in an affirming, nonracist way. By returning to the source, Diop's anthropological and archaeological investigation led him to write *The African Origin of Civilization* (1974), which challenged the cultural and historical defamation of Africa and her people. What Diop essentially did conceptually was to challenge the Eurocentric evolutionist belief in the progressive movement of humanity from barbarianism to civilization by proving that in the case of Africa, African people had been forced to move from civilization into the barbaric worlds of the Europeans and Arabo-Semitic people. He further saw that a cultural similitude existed among African people, which led to findings that revealed that cultural unity was possible. Not unlike Marcus Garvey, Diop believed that African cultural unity could be nurtured as a way of not only restoring the dignity of Africa and her people but also creating an African renaissance in rebuilding Africa. Similarly, Hilliard and Williams (1987) reintroduced the work of Ptahhotep, the first philosopher, to underscore the primacy of African origin. Fundamental to the restoration of cultural unity was the necessary development of a cultural identity. Diop (2011) believed that African cultural identity could be shaped and realized through the components of history, language, psychology, and spirituality so vital to creating a collective identity.

The historical factor is the cultural glue that unifies a community with a sense of belonging. The collective experience over time is part of the historical continuity that is spiritually connected to the ancestors, who are remembered for their positive contribution to family, society, nation, state, and the world. Through communion with the ancestors, history provides a consciousness that enables people to identify themselves as part of a population connected in ways that define their traditional similarities and distinctions from other cultural groups. Individual members of cultural groups desire to know, understand, appreciate, and live their historical legacy and transmit their cultural memory, or heritage, to their descendants (Dove, 2015b).

Psychology, the study of the human mind and behavior, derives from the Greek word *psyche*, itself rooted in its ancient African antecedent *sakhu*, essentially the "soul of being." It underpins the development of identity, personality, and consciousness. The study of the human mind and behavior cannot be separated from an exploration of matters of the spirit as they shape concepts of humanity and understandings of "self." Humans want to be loved and appreciated and respected as they grow to understand the collective ideals from prebirth to adulthood. In this way, they can locate themselves, fulfil their potential, and contribute to their own and their society's future (Dove, 2015a).

Language, as sound and vibrational forces, is emitted to the *sakhu*, the soul of being. This emission is a valuable cohesive base for cultural identity and unity, enabling the exchange and passing of knowledge to specifically enhance existence and connectivity. It transmits thoughts, ideals, hopes, aspirations, values, beliefs, and directives, also conveying musical expressions that can evoke all manner of emotional states, movements, and behaviors enabling life, healing, disease, and death (Dove, 2015b).

As a powerful purveyor of ideas, values, and beliefs, culture aids in the shaping of human thoughts and behavior. It provides a reservoir of information grounded in experiences that act as a foundation for making sense of life and how it may be lived. It affects decisions and actions in the methods employed to build social institutions like family, health care, education, politics, economies, entertainment, the arts, and spiritual systems (Dove, 2015b).

In reference to knowledge development, episteme is equally culturally grounded. It is the knowledge gained through the historical, linguistic, psychological, and spiritual experiences of people. Episteme, knowledge, affects the shaping of the mind, and the mind affects the shaping of the knowledge and therefore culture. Each cultural group over time comes to regard its knowledge as true. Knowledge should be based on truth so that it will sustain the culture in which it arises. In this light, epistemology is the philosophical study of knowledge and questions why we think the way we do and why we believe what we believe. It interrogates the source of knowledge, thereby questioning the study of origins and therefore the study of humanity from the distant past until now.

The theory of knowledge is grounded foremost in trying to understand the secrets of the universe and requires specialized training to achieve higher learning. Essentially, there are two paths for seeking knowledge. One path will lead to truth (Ma'at), and the other will lead to knowledge of the opinions of women and men (James, 1989). The Western focus on knowledge is relative to the perceptions of the seeker. We understand that Greeks went to Africa to go through a specialized training to seek higher knowledge. In this case, knowledge and truth, like the seeker, are culturally grounded. The search for knowledge is tempered and shaped by cultures that differ in their political, religious, and scientific objectives. In ancient African higher learning, the spiritual, political, and scientific are harmonious; the objective is to live in Ma'at (truth, justice, reciprocity, and harmony), an Ancient Africa–wide belief that was crystalized and codified in Kemet (Ancient Egypt).

Afrocentric theory is grounded in an African *sebayet* (wisdom) that is based on the truth of human history, which began in Africa, and as such opposes the false narratives of Africa and her people grounded in the construction of race. Afrocentric theory is therefore regarded as a danger to the most prominent epistemes that consider the more melaninated people of African descent genetically inferior and in some cases subhuman. Even in the realization of the reality that African (black) or First Nations (red) women, men, and children are not inferior, there are still ongoing attempts to use racist epistemes, whether religious or academic, as possible routes to achieving antiracist liberation. When choosing avenues that lead to truth, epistemes should be investigated in relation to where African women, men, and children are placed in theories and stories, particularly those pertaining to creation.

An important feature of episteme is logic. The logos and the logic are connected to the mind, informed by thought, with the emission of harmonious sound becoming the creative energy from which logic arises. Logic is linked to truth, the source of life. In this way, logic and truth are inexorably bound. Logic is used as a way to judge the truth of a theory and the explanation of what is proposed or inferred as reality. Humans are able to use logic to understand whether the sounds or utterances of speech as language are true.

Some have questioned Diop's (1989) use of "black" Africa in his work *The Cultural Unity of Black Africa*, which defines the roots of African matriarchy and Indo-Aryan-European and Arab-Semitic patriarchy. Diop places emphasis on highlighting the cultural distinctions among humanity as the basis for human development and difference. He is clear that the first people in the world, who developed the first culture, were highly pigmented with melanin and these black African women, men, and children were the progenitors of *Homo sapiens*, today's anatomical humans. Thus, although some *Homo sapiens* left Africa 70,000 years ago, we have been in existence for at least 250,000 to 300,000 years, creating monuments and civilizations prior to coming out of Africa (Diop, 1992; Hilliard, 1998; National Geographic, 2018). In agreement with Diop, Asante (2019) in *The History of Africa: The Quest for Eternal Harmony* noted that the pioneering work of Diop claiming that Africa was the home of civilization and humanity and that Europe had stolen and distorted much of the African record brought with it a wave of intellectual resistance that would follow Diop for most of his life because he challenged the idea of European superiority. Since then, more evidence has accrued from disciplines as varied as archaeology and linguistics that has proved his work to be true. In fact, Africa is the source of many of the technological innovations that laid the foundation for modern industrial and informational societies (Asante, 2019).

It is from scientific knowledge that we know that we are one human race, which effectively obliterates the racial paradigm that has imposed a baseless idea that humans evolved as genetically different races in different areas of the world. Others have had no problem with humanity leaving Africa but have suggested through the theory of evolution that the changing phenotypes denote superior and inferior traits based on skin color. In this way, race has been a genetic blight on black-skinned humanity from its inception, as defined and suggested in religious beliefs and texts like the Rig Veda, the Tanakh, the Bible, and the Quran. The formulation of the inferiority of African/black women, men, and children in sacred beliefs is codified as a perceived reality. This codification of race is in reality founded on a clever, devious lie that focuses on difference as genetically determined. As a result, countless millions of the African people who remained in Africa and millions of those who left have been enslaved and murdered under the vile belief, which is still current, that people of African descent, especially those of the darkest hue and with the most melanin, are deserving of enslavement, genocide, mistreatment, abuse, defamation, destruction, demonization, debasement, murder, torture, and annihilation by any means necessary by the perpetrators and believers in race, the hierarchy of humanity. In using the idea that these human behaviors are inhuman, we use the set of standards developed in Africa, called Ma'at in Kemet, that evaluate what it is to become civilized. For example, for African-descended people living in the Americas, in racist environments where there is overrepresentation of black women, men, and children in prisons, mental health institutions, and poor neighborhoods, and police killings are rampant, it is difficult to speak of justice. In Western culture, there is talk of justice, but the original idea is African because Ma'at is the source of reciprocity. Through Asante's Afrocentric theory, the episteme that uses African reality as the portal through which African humanity is treasured, it has been possible to reawaken African cultural memory and legacy in the effort to return us to normality about who we are and why we are here.

Diop's focus on the significance of culture to life brings culture to the forefront of making sense of human behavior. Tracing cultural antecedents to their roots, Diop found that distinctions among ways of conducting life and developing morals and ethics, values, beliefs, and behaviors related primarily to the arrangements of female–male power relations, the smallest unit of family, society, nation, and civilization, who are the source of the procreation of life, culture, and development. African matriarchy is the first culture that rose out of Africa and is a complex, gendered social order that evolved from the reciprocal, balanced, egalitarian, and democratic relationship between the woman and the man. This balanced, just relationship produced families, societies, and nations that sought Ma'at—order, reciprocity, harmony, love, truth, justice, and peace—the basis of true democracy and the foundation of higher learning.

Matriarchy is not an absolute and cynical triumph of woman over man; it is a harmonious dualism, an association accepted by both sexes, the better to build a sedentary society where each and every one could fully develop by following the activity best suited to their physiological nature. A matriarchal regime, far from being imposed on man by circumstances independent of his will, is accepted and defended by him. (Diop, 2000).

Those African women, men, and children who left Africa 70,000 years ago left with the first culture based on female and male reciprocity. Some of the earliest African civilizations were founded on African matriarchy, an important feature of which is xenophilia, the love of humanity. Kemet was one such civilization.

Over thousands of years, phenotypes changed, and those African women, men, and children who survived the harsher climes and lost their melanin forgot their ancient ancestors. Owing to harsh climes, particularly in the north, it is surmised that these men and women became patriarchal, whereby the man dominated the woman. This was the first hierarchy of injustice that was reflected in the family, society, nation, and civilization, where man was considered superior to woman.

This relationship is founded on a lie as woman is not inferior to man. From this first injustice comes *Isfet*, the opposite of Ma'at: chaos, lies, disharmony, hate, aggression, domination, and war. Moreover, these characteristics are features of xenophobia, the fear of others. This unjust relationship is the total antithesis of female and male reciprocity. For this reason, these cultural groups continue to stand in direct opposition to each other.

Diop (1974) attributes these cultural differences in African matriarchy to the agrarian lifestyle in a climate of abundance and European/Indo-Aryan patriarchy to nomadic traditions arising from a harsh environment. In time, patriarchal culture would develop instincts necessary for survival in such an environment. Man must obtain his bread by the sweat of his brow. Above all, he must learn to rely on himself alone. He could not indulge in the luxury of believing in a beneficent God who would shower down abundant means of gaining a livelihood; instead, he would conjure up deities maleficent and cruel, jealous and spiteful: Zeus and Yahweh, among others.

Within patriarchy, as Diop (1992) further explains, the European or Indo-Aryan woman is considered little more than a burden that the man drags behind him. Beyond her function of childbearing, her role is nothing. As a person of lesser value, she must join her husband's family to join her husband, unlike the matriarchal custom that requires the man to join his wife's family (Diop, 2000).

In contradiction, the concept of African matriarchy highlights the complementary aspect of the female–male relationship or the nature of the feminine and masculine in all aspects of social organization. The woman is revered in her role as the mother who is the bringer of life, the conduit to the spiritual regeneration of the ancestors, the bearer of culture, and the center of social organization. According to Diop, to speak or behave inappropriately in front of a mother is tantamount to committing sacrilege. It is believed that such behavior will be known in the ancestors' realm, and

Patriarchy: The Origin of Hierarchy and Race

the repercussions will fall on the families of the perpetrators. As a result of her powerful role, the mother wishes to use her power wisely and will often be tolerant toward her children and her partner (Diop, 1990). In the environment of Western patriarchy, this tolerance may be exploited and viewed as a weakness rather than a strength. The act of mothering is not restricted to mothers or women even in contemporary Africa (Tedla, 1995). Motherhood depicts the nature of communal responsibilities in the raising of children and the caring of others. This belief was no more highly regarded than during enslavement in the Americas, when survival was reliant on the compassion and care of every African person enslaved.

Amadiume (1962/2000), in her tribute to Diop in the Foreword of Diop's book *The Cultural Unity of Black Africa*, speculated that there is always the tendency for man to dominate woman, which in relation to colonial Africa makes sense as patriarchal cultural conquest and domination have done a lot to destroy and corrupt the more ancient African matriarchy embedded in deep structure (see also Amadiume, 1987b). It is found that the present tendency of the internal evolution of the African family is toward a patriarchy more or less attenuated by the matriarchal origins of the society. We cannot emphasize too much the role played in this transformation by outside factors, such as the religions of Islam and Christianity and the secular presence of Europe in Africa (Diop, 2000).

The idea of the "zone of confluence" in Diop's analysis of cultural distinctions highlights what happens when these opposing cultures meet. African matriarchy is recognized as the oldest culture. Patriarchy, the younger culture whose creators lost touch with their ancestors, returned to Africa as a conquering force led by Indo-Aryans, now less pigmented. They arrived in the areas that dark-skinned African people still populated. Like the cuckoo, which seeks the comfort of usurping another bird's nest to lay its own eggs, throwing out the builders and babies and planting itself in the middle of the nest, the nomadic Indo-Aryans, without knowing that they were meeting their own ancestors, conquered areas rich in knowledge and abundant in agriculture and minerals, which later became known as Arabia, Southwest Asia, the Middle East, and India. Consequently, and ironically, African, deeply melaninated black women are not only the mothers of humanity but, much later, became the mothers of the Arabic/Semitic people, the amalgamation of the Indo-Aryan and African. In this zone of confluence, usually a zone of conquest, the children decided whether to follow the mothers' cultural tradition or that of their fathers. As Chancellor Williams (1992) argues, the children of this amalgamation, essentially the Semitic fathers labeled Caucasian/Asian and African mothers, took great care to distinguish themselves from Africans. This "new breed" joined their fathers and forefathers in the wars and enslaving raids against the blacks until the whole of North Africa was eventually taken.

Although phenotypes changed over time, cultures did not necessarily change, so it is entirely possible to find African matriarchal values and beliefs still existing in societies not considered African—such as the First Nation Kayapo women, men, and children of Brazil, who are facing genocide being terrorized by the Portuguese; the Taino, First Nation people of Ayiti; the First Nation people in Australia; and the Haida First Nation people in British Columbia.

All institutions, the social pillars of societies, are shaped and formed by culture, such as family, health care, education, politics, economies, spiritual systems, and entertainment. It is in this regard that we can then understand that, for example, political systems are fashioned by the people who develop them—as in the case of European, Arabo-Semitic, and Indian political institutions, which are patriarchal and racist, believing in the inferiority of black women, men, and children. Within their political systems, the woman barely has any ministerial roles, and if she is enabled to do so, she is essentially commandeering a patriarchal/racist political system. She is often guilty, as in the case of Margaret Thatcher, prime minister of England from 1979 to 1990, famously known as the

"Iron Lady," who made financial cutbacks on free school milk for already impoverished families (both black and white), began the privatization of free health, supported police brutality against black youth, and started a war with Argentina. In all these cases, women as mothers, families, and children suffered incredibly.

Another example of institutional development are the spiritual systems in many locations in Africa, where women's power is critical in both physical and spiritual forms to maintain balance and harmony among members of the society (Afua, 2001; Dorsey, 2020). Wherever Africa was conquered by patriarchs, for example, Arabo-Semites and Europeans, they imposed religions, such as Christianity and Islam, rooted in Hebrew teachings whereby the woman is perceived to be of less value than the man in the physical and spiritual realms. As a result of the primacy given to women's power in African traditional systems, they were debased and banned by the patriarchal conquerors as they were perceived as a source of contention.

In 325 CE, Constantine, the first emperor of Rome, ruled his empire, which included Egypt, from his capital Byzantium, which he renamed Constantinople. He convened the First Council of Nicea in Turkey. His ultimate plan was to be worshipped as God. He is said to have had visions of God and the symbol of the cross, which led to his conversion to Christianity. He claimed that God spoke through him, so he came to be viewed by the doubting Christians as omnipotent (Grant, 1993). In this process, the emperor gathered together the official religious leaders, many of whom still believed in the powers of their divinities, and through promises of wealth and power, he inveigled them to accept Christianity as the official religion that would override all the others. His Christian idea of God, the Father and Son, met with resistance by those Greeks, Romans, and Africans whose names and attributes for the divine preexisted Christianity.

The major problem for Constantine was posed by Arius, a member of the Coptic Church, who asked, "How could the son (Jesus) be considered a divinity like the father (God) and yet be recognized as human?" Up until then, divinities were of the spirit. This raised questions about how the son came into existence (Grant, 1993; Williams, 1992). Clearly, the Council of Nicea established the idea that God, Jesus, and the Holy Ghost were equal parts of the Holy Trinity. Jesus was said to be fully divine and fully human, although this was not settled completely until the Council of Ephesus in 431 CE. In introducing the idea of a solution, the council took the woman out of the triad, as had been the case in ancient African religion, and replaced her with the Holy Ghost. The divinity of Jesus did not have to compete with that of Mary or of any other woman; only Jesus was incarnate as both human and divine. Arianism was banished and essentially cast out of the Roman Christian doctrine. At the same time, the council confirmed patriarchy and the inferiority of the African woman by removing the need for women's representation in the triad. In this way, Constantine could be worshipped as God, and Mary, the mother of Jesus, was relegated to the vessel within which this divine spirit incubated because she was immaculately conceived. Constantine declared Christianity the official state religion in 333 CE. Pre-Christian beliefs held by Romans, Greeks, and others, including Kemetic spirituality, were demoted as pagan and viewed with disdain, a belief still in effect today. Years later, the Christian emperor Theodosius's decision to close down all the temples in Egypt in 391 CE was reinforced in 527 CE by the Christian emperor Justinian and again by the Arabs with Islam in 642 CE (Browder, 1992). The closure of Kemetic temples can be related to the banning of African matriarchal beliefs, where women held key roles. Such actions continue to be reinforced today. The first purveyor of sin in the Hebrew (Semitic) creation story is Eve, the first woman, who would have to be a reference to the African mother of humanity since *Homo sapiens* arose in Africa.

While it is important to look at patriarchy as a cultural construction that has undermined African matriarchy, our argument and logic go further to explain that, in fact, patriarchy is the foundation of and fundamental to the belief in human hierarchy. It is not much of a stretch to understand how the domination of a person to compel her to carry out the tasks that her servility requires can provide the man with the time to do something for himself. In this way, individualism, superiority, indolence, materialism, and greed can manifest. It so happens that they are the primary principles of capitalism, viewed theoretically as having evolved around the time of the Industrial Revolution during the 1700s, based and dependent on the wealth accrued from the enslavement of African women, men, and children. When investigating the emergence of the hierarchy of humanity, one might argue that these burgeoning cultural manifestations of greed, individualism, sloth, materialism, and superiority are integral to these patriarchal beliefs. The African priest and philosopher Ptahhotep said 4,500 years ago,

> If you want to have perfect conduct, to be free from every evil, then above all guard against the vice of greed. Greed is a grievous sickness that has no cure. There is no treatment for it. It embroils fathers, mothers and the brothers of the mother. It parts the wife from the husband. Greed is a compound of all evils. It is a bundle of hateful things. That person endures whose rule is righteous, who walks a straight line, for that person will leave a legacy by such behavior. On the other hand, the greedy has no tomb. (Hilliard & Williams, 1987, p. 25)

This is not for us to imagine that humans are unaffected by greed as it is a human failing. However, it can be said that patriarchal hierarchy fundamentally produces these behaviors, which are not curbed and in reality are rather promoted, as evidenced in the conquest of the world. Thus, broadened by xenophobia, the fear of "other" people, societies, nations, and civilizations, the tendency for aggression, conquest, and domination that patriarchs exhibit makes this hierarchy achievable.

Early evidence of this can be traced to Kemet when the Hyksos, Assyrians, Persians, Greeks, Romans, Turks and Arabs, all patriarchs, conquered and robbed its wealth of knowledge and cultural abundance. These patriarchs, like cuckoos seeking new nests, attempted to take African civilization as their own, basking in its light, without the historical or herstorical knowledge, training, or experience to produce that light or even understand it. Each one of these conquering patriarchs recognized that they were in Africa, more specifically Kushite or even Nubian territory, and that the abundance that they craved and the knowledge that they plagiarized was African and black. We see this reality in the paintings from the tomb of Rameses 111 (1200 BCE), where Egyptians saw themselves as African and black and painted themselves as such, identifying themselves with other Africans and distinguishing themselves from Indo-Europeans and Semites, clearly showing the phenotypical differences in *Egypt Revisited* (Van Sertima, 1983; see also Diop, 1989).

References and Notes

Afua, Q. (2001). *Sacred lady*. Random House.

Amadiume, I. (1987a). *Afrikan matriarchal foundations: The Igbo case*. Karnak House.

    Amadiume is one of the pioneers of the discourse around African women.

Amadiume, I. (1987b). *Male daughters, female husbands: Gender and sex in an African society*. Zed Books.

Amadiume, I. (1992). *Male daughters, female husbands: Gender and sex in an African society* (3rd ed.). Zed Books.

Amadiume, I. (2000). Foreword. In C. A. Diop, *The cultural unity of black Africa: The domains of matriarchy and of patriarchy in classical antiquity*. Karnak House. (Original work published 1962)

    Amadiume established herself in the history of the discourse on matriarchy by bringing to the forefront the African perspective on this subject in light of Diop's original arguments.

Aptheker, H. (1975). *A documentary history of the Negro peoples* (2 vols.). Carol Publishing. (Original work published 1951)

Asante, M. K. (1987). *The Afrocentric idea*. Temple University Press.

> In this book, Asante introduces a new epistemic position called Afrocentricity, where studies of African phenomena would place Africans in the center of their narrative. The idea is centrality to one's history, not marginality. Here, Asante traces the remarkable resilience of Africans in the United States by asserting agency despite the oppositional attitudes of whites.

Asante, M. K. (2018). *The American demagogue: Donald Trump in the American presidency*. Universal Write.

> This was the first book to be published after Trump's election that tied his style, methods, rhetoric, and bombast to the history of American racial demagoguery. Here, Asante claims that Trump saw himself in line with the bombastic demagogues who appealed to many racist whites as their leader, much like the southern demagogues had done during the most violent and bleak period in American history around 1880 to 1925. Asante's work, based on communication theory, exposed Trump's tools of crowd control to build a cult movement around his personality.

Asante, M. K. (2019). *The history of Africa: The quest for eternal harmony*. Routledge. https://doi.org/10.4324/9781315168166

> One of the first comprehensive histories of the African continent written by an African. In this book, Asante follows the philosophical and historiographical tradition of the best African historians in relationship to antiquity, fellowship, family relations, and movement of the African people throughout the world.

Beauvoir, S. de. (2011). *The second sex*. Vintage Books, 2011.

Bernal, M. (2006). *Black Athena: Afroasiatic roots of classical civilization*. Rutgers University Press.

> What Bernal emphatically argued was that the Greek ideas were found earlier in Africa and Asia. He was particularly interested in how the Greeks took many of their ideas from African and Hebraic influences, especially from the Nile Valley and the Southwest Asian regions of the ancient world.

Browder, A. T. (1992). *Nile Valley contributions to civilization: Exploding the myths*. Karmic Guidance.

> Browder provides a brilliant accounting of the many African contributions to world civilization, showing how Africa has influenced many contemporary aspects of society.

Chandler, W. B. (1999). *Ancient future: The teachings and prophetic wisdom of the Seven Hermetic Laws of Ancient Egypt*. Black Classic Press.

Claire, M. (2021, January 7). *Trump's mob attacked the Capitol—but democracy was their real target*. https://www.marieclaire.com/politics/a35142183/trump-capitol-riot-essay-mikki-kendall/

> This article shows that the target of the rioters and insurrectionists was really the idea of democracy. They believed the lie that the election had been stolen, although all legitimate institutions of news and information had declared Biden the winner over Trump. The mob wanted Vice President Pence to stop the certifying of the electoral college votes. They felt that Pence had betrayed their interests by saying that he would fulfill his constitutional responsibilities. January 6, 2021, remains an iconic date in American history because it was the day American democracy was saved by the brave men and women who after the riot had subsided went back to the Capitol and certified the votes.

Curry, T. J. (2017). *The man, not: Race, class, genre and the dilemmas of Black manhood.* Temple University Press.

> Curry proves that the image of the African as a predator is incorrect given the evolution of white fear and rage at the black male body. We take the position that Adebayo Oluwayomi argues in the *Journal of Men's Studies*, where he claims that one must not read Curry's work as intersectionality. In "The Man-Not and the Inapplicability of Intersectionality to the Dilemmas of Black Manhood," published in January 2020, Oluwayomi argues that Curry is more interested in black male victimization than in a reading of intersectionality.

Diop, C. A. (1974). *The African origin of civilization.* Lawrence Hill.

> The reader must read this entire classic book for a full understanding of the intellectual transformation that was created by Diop between 1948 and 1980.

Diop, C. A. (1989). *The cultural unity of black Africa.* Karnak House.

Diop, C. A. (1992). *Civilization or barbarism: An authentic anthropology* (Y.-L. M. Ngemi, Trans.). Chicago Review Press.

Diop, C. A. (2000). *The cultural unity of black Africa: The domains of matriarchy and of patriarchy in classical antiquity.* Karnak House.

> Here is Diop's penetrating examination of patriarchy and matriarchy.

Dorsey, L. (2020). *Orishas, goddesses, and voodoo queens: The divine feminine in the African religious traditions.* Weiser.

Dove, N. (1994). The emergence of black supplementary schools as forms of resistance to racism in the United Kingdom. In M. J. Shujaa (Ed.), *Too much schooling, too little education: A paradox of black life in white society* (pp. 343–360). Africa World Press.

Dove, N. (1995). An African centered critique of Marx's logic. *Western Journal of Black Studies, 19*(3), 260–271.

Dove, N. (1998). *Afrikan mothers: Bearers of culture, makers of social change.* SUNY Press.

Dove, N. (2015a). Cultural imperialism. In M. J. Shujaa & K. J. Shujaa (Eds.), *The SAGE encyclopedia of African cultural heritage in North America.* Sage.

Dove, N. (2015b). Matriarchy and patriarchy. In M. J. Shujaa & K. J. Shujaa (Eds.), *The SAGE encyclopedia of African cultural heritage in North America*. Sage.

Feagin, J. R. (2006). *Systemic racism: A theory of oppression*. Routledge.

Grant, M. (1993). *The Emperor Constantine*. Weidenfeld & Nicolson.

Hilliard, A. G., III. (1998). *SBA: The reawakening of the African mind*. Makare.

Hilliard, A. G., III, & Williams, L. (1987). *The teachings of Ptahhotep: The oldest book in the world*. Blackwood Press.

James, G. G. M. (1989). *Stolen legacy*. Africa World Press.

When Martin Bernal was asked about this book, he claimed that it had deliberately been made invisible in the tradition of European historical thought. Alongside Asa Hilliard, Jacob Carruthers, and Molefi Kete Asante, Bernal revived the reading of George G. M. James's book. Actually, James was one of the early Guyanese scholars who added to a powerful school of thought with Ivan Van Sertima, Kimani Nehusi, and Walter Rodney, among others.

Karenga, M. (2006). *Maat: The moral ideal in Ancient Egypt*. University of Sankore Press.

This book is the monumental work of one of the contemporary giants in ancient Kemetic studies. One cannot know the African understanding of Ma'at without a close reading of Karenga's work.

Levinas, E. (1987). *Time and the other* (R. A. Cohen, Trans.). Duquesne University Press.

Lorde, A. (2018). *The master's tools will never dismantle the master's house*. Penguin Random House.

One of the key voices on issues of gender and eroticism in contemporary society.

National Geographic. (2018, April). The race issue: These twins will make you rethink race. *National Geographic Magazine*. https://www.nationalgeographic.com/magazine/issue/april-2018

Olivelle, P. (2005). Laws of Manu. In *Manu's code of law: A critical edition and translation of the Mānava-Dharmaśāstra*. Oxford University Press.

Oyěwùmí, O. (1997). *Invention of women: Making an African sense of Western gender discourses* (Kindle ed.). University of Minnesota Press.

Parker, K., Morin, R., & Horowitz, J. M. (2019, March 21). *Looking to the future, public sees an America in decline on many fronts: Views of demographic change*. Pew Research Center.

Rashidi, R. (2017). *My global journeys in search of African presence*. Black Classic Press.

Rashidi R., & Van Sertima, I. (1988). *African presence in early Asia*. Transaction.

Tedla, E. (1995). *Sankofa: African thought and education*. Peter Lang.

Van Sertima, I. (1976). *They came before Columbus*. Random House.

> Van Sertima writes about the Malian emperor who sent more than 1,000 long boats across the ocean on a journey from Africa, and when they did not return, he took another 1,000 the next year and disappeared in the ocean. Evidence that these sailors landed in the Americas was demonstrated by Van Sertima with studies of cotton; the folktales of the Amerindians created controversy but were supported by the medieval history of the kingdom of Mali, the earlier book by Leo Wiener, and writings by other scholars who pointed out the Nubian appearance of many of the Olmec sculptures.

Van Sertima, I. (1983). *Egypt revisited*. Transaction.

Walker, R. (2006). *When we ruled: The ancient and medieval history of black civilizations*. Every Generation Media.

Williams, C. (1992). *The destruction of black civilization*. Third World Press.

> Williams's book remains one of the most influential in the African American community among cultural and social scholars interested in the historical moment that ushered in the invasions that undercut the authorial institutions on the African continent.

Woodson, C. G. (1933). *The miseducation of the Negro*. Standard.

Yellen, J. E., Brooks, A. S., Cornelissen, E., Mehlman, M. J., & Stewart, K. (1995). A Middle Stone Age worked bone industry from Katanda, Upper Semliki Valley, Zaire. *Science*, *268*(5210), 553–556. https://doi.org/10.1126/science.7725100

CHAPTER 2

Race and Culture

The word "race" was used for centuries to refer to what are now called ethnic groups in the West and in parts of Asia. In fact, one often reads of the Ethiopian race, the Persian race, the Bedouin race, and so forth. However, the word became more related to phenotype after the 18th century. Thus, as Bernard Lewis (1990) noted, a word commonly used took on specific uses in the minds of Western social scientists. Chief among these social scientists were anthropologists who tried to classify human beings as botanists had classified plants and biologists had classified animals. Hence, physical traits like the color of the skin, width of the nose, texture of the hair, and measurement of skulls became marks of different races. This system carried inside it its own inherent contradictions because people of the same ancestral family could be classified into different races. Where the West had spoken of the German race, the Italian race, or the English race, its writers eventually during the 19th century abandoned "race" for terms like "nation," "ethnic group," or "people." "Race" was reserved for use in reference to large groups of people who one could *see* were different in some physical manner. Language, habits, traditions, and customs hardly mattered so long as the physical characteristics could be described in a certain way.

The evolution of the term, or we should say the evolution of the discussion about the term "race," meant that something with no biological, that is, scientific, base had to be looked on by social scientists and students of culture as an illusion. Ultimately, it would be revealed for what it was in terms of hegemony and hierarchy. All classification becomes an instrument for organizing and managing large classes of things, including people. Europeans following others, as we should see, found a novel approach to such hierarchical idea of control.

Race is a cultural construction and is in fact a falsehood constructed by patriarchs. We highlight the creation of race and race identity in their popularly used sense by European, Indo-Aryan (white), Southwest Asian (often misnamed Middle Eastern), and Semitic men and women, whose cultural construction of race was sanctioned by religious ideals that advanced their societies and stigmatized African humanity based on the melanin content of their skin. In these cultural orientations, the blackest-skinned women, men, and children are devalued, debased, and demonized. The current situation is that these "dominant" cultures have been imposed on African people from the continent wherever the diaspora live in the world, whether Europe, the Americas, Australia, or Asia. In this way, women, men, and children live in and are "nurtured" by cultures that demean and debase African humanity. Furthermore, the victims of these lies are taught through a "schooling" process, a concept developed by Mwalimu Shujaa (1998) to distinguish it from education, which is a cultural process of learning based on truth, growing, and becoming. In the United States, one can speak of African Americans existing within the social and historical context of the state, but Africans in America predate the nation-state because of the continuum that would exist even if the nation-state disappeared (Shujaa, 1998). Thus, we agree with Shujaa that through schooling we learn how to accept and even participate in the racialization and demonization of self and others like ourselves.

It is not difficult to come to the conclusion that the domination of woman by man, recognized as the first injustice and the first hierarchy, leads to the belief that hierarchy is beneficial. In time, the woman and man in this arrangement were able to collaborate in and fashion a pattern of perceiving and instituting a hierarchy of humanity based on their own hierarchical relationship to each other, which justified their domination of others. The "inferiorizing" of the woman was the first step down the treacherous road of both patriarchy and hierarchy. Domination was the first act of terror.

The early patriarchal cultures, the Hyksos, Persians, Assyrians, Greeks, Romans, and Arabs, had a common purpose in hating and inferiorizing darker-skinned women, men, and children. They wanted what African women, men, and children had, by any means necessary. The creation of the illusion of race was a necessary prerequisite for attainment of control and authority over Africans. In fact, Chinweizu (2010), the famous Nigerian philosopher, claims that Europe's race war on Africans started when the captains of two of Prince Henry's (of Portugal) exploring caravels brought back with them to Lisbon in 1442 a dozen Africans, whom they had captured on the west coast in the course of a wholly unprovoked attack on an African village. Further exploits of a similar kind followed. Not long after that, Pope Nicholas V (1447–1455) spelled out and blessed a war, in the name of Christ, on the world's non-Christian peoples:

> "We, after scrupulous reflection, are granting by our Bull full and entire freedom to King Alphonso [of Spain] to conquer, to besiege, to fight, and to submit all the Saracens, Pagans, and other enemies of Christ, wherever they may be; and to seize the kingdoms, the dukedoms, the princedoms, the lordships, personal properties, landed properties, and all the wealth they withhold and possess;

and to submit these persons to a perpetual slavery; to appropriate these kingdoms, duchies, principalities, counties, lordships, properties and wealth; to transmit them to their successors; to take advantage and make use of them personally and with their offspring." (Ngubane, 1979, pp. 44–45)

What is clear in the statements of Chinweizu and Ngubane is that the pope, the head of the Roman Catholic Church, authorized the commitment of crimes and mortal sins against all people not considered Christians. In fact, the division of the world into Portuguese and Spanish spheres was linked with slavery, colonialism, racism, segregation, and apartheid. Pope Alexander's Bull *Inter Caetera* of 1493 divided all the heathens of the world with their resources between Portugal and Spain. And later, Pope Clement VI in *Intra Arcana*, the Bull he issued on May 8, 1529, and addressed to Charles V of Spain, urged him on to war with the heathens, saying,

"We trust that, as long as you are on earth, you will compel and with all zeal cause the barbarian nations to come to the knowledge of God, the maker and founder of all things, not only by edicts and admonitions, but also by force and arms, if needful, in order that their souls may partake of the heavenly kingdom." (Ngubane, 1979, pp. 44–45)

Clearly, the war against Africans in particular lasted deep into the 20th century and is still not completely settled as Europe's global race war, declared by Europe in religious terms, is also led by nations such as the United States and Australia.

European Culture and Race

By the 1700s, a serious European academic effort, known as the Pan-European Academy, was embarked on to prove scientifically that humans are distinctly different largely based on skin color. This pseudoscientific effort was underpinned by the reality of the enslavement of people of African descent. The argument was that differences could be discerned basically from the amount of melanin in the skin, which determined the level of genetic inferiority and superiority related to culture, intelligence, psychology, mental attributes, spirituality, moral characteristics, physical prowess, linguistics, behaviors, and so on. The use of the comparative research methodology was made popular. Its proponents, drawing on their own cultural beliefs, officially placed the white or Caucasian man and woman at the top of a race hierarchy of humanity. This comprehensive doctrine was used to justify white control over non-white people, the atrocities of the enslavement of countless millions of African people, as well as the appropriation of land and resources, including knowledge and energy (Dove, 2015).

Racial Ladder

Europe had developed a system of typology to classify nature. What was called typological thinking about race, however, was really hierarchical thinking about race. This hierarchy we refer to as the racial ladder. It is embedded in the distorted and often malicious science of European writers bent on "proving" their superiority to other people. It was then and is now an illusion. It is possible to say that the racial ladder illusion started in the 18th and into the 20th century, when many "scientists" of Europe and America began to write detailed accounts of their studies of humanity. Of course, during the time of the enslavement of Africans and the colonization of much of the world by Europe, the "science" had already been distorted by the self-importance of the conquerors. The idea was to seek documentation for what they considered to be the superiority of whites and the inferiority of all other people. The construction and propagation of this illusion dominated the churches, schools, legislatures, courts, and libraries until throughout the world of Europe and America the idea that whites were divinely chosen to be at the top of the racial ladder became almost universal. Furthermore, Edward Long (1734–1813), a plantation owner in Jamaica, published *The History of Jamaica* (1774/2011), in which he argued that African people were incapable of civilization. Long's book was used as a defense for the enslavement of Africans because the idea of slavery being the lot of the African was a meme already in the thinking of many white people.

A few years after Long's book was published, a physician from Manchester, England, named Charles White in 1799 wrote a description of human races. His description of each racial category started with the head and then considered all physical aspects of people, such as the feet, arms, complexion, hair texture, and ability to combat or catch diseases. His position, like that of other racial scientists, was that white people were the most civilized since they had made progress from the Garden of Eden and Africans, Asians, and American Indian people had only degenerated toward savagery. Blumenbach (1795/1969) identified five types of races, which he called Caucasian, Mongolian, Ethiopian, American, and Malay. He regarded the Caucasian form of the skull "the most beautiful in the human spectrum" and believed that there was reason to accept it as representing the original human form, declaring that "white … we may fairly assume to have been the primitive colour of mankind" (p. 269). Almost no "scientist" was as critical to the promotion of the racial ladder as the Philadelphia physician and anatomist Samuel George Morton (1799–1851), who wrote *Crania Americana* in 1839. It was Morton who called Blumenbach's five categories "races" and used similar descriptive terms for each of the five groups as did Blumenbach. In effect, the American Morton pioneered the use of the racial ladder in the United States and made it the fundamental lever for the fulcrum of racism in the American South. White southerners considered Morton, the scientist, an authority on the nature of races. Additional negative and pejorative descriptions of Africans continued from one writer to the next until the picture of the racial ladder appeared quite clearly from the collective writings of Linnaeus, Blumenbach, Morton, and Buffon, among others:

The Racial Ladder
European: Beautiful, handsome, sanguine, civilized
Mongolian: Inscrutable, melancholy
Malay: Sad, rigid
American Indian: Immutably irascible
Ethiopian: Intrinsically savage, ugly, lazy

What is immediately obvious is that this racial ladder was the work of white people. Its unflattering description of blacks and other people shows that it was intended to degrade black people. As we shall see, the European thoughts about race are grounded in a distorted concept of evolution, developed most prominently by Charles Darwin (1859/1982), who was, according to Gould (1981), "a kindly, liberal, passionate abolitionist," as shown in his book *The Voyage of the Beagle* (1839/2014) and by his disgust with a neighbor, an elderly woman who kept screws to crush the fingers of her "female slaves." He narrated his abhorrence of other heinous crimes that he witnessed, committed by Europeans against enslaved African children, women, and men, yet although he questioned how they could believe in the teachings of Christianity and profess to love God, he firmly believed in the inferiority of African people. One cannot help but wonder what was the moral compass that he used to both define inferiority and superiority and judge himself.

In answer to this question, one would have to draw on the widespread effects of the Christian belief in the inferiority of African/black humanity, which shall be explained in the section on the construction of race in Semitic, Middle Eastern beliefs. However, while Darwin's book *The Descent of Man* (1871/1981) reflected biblical ideas espousing the racialization of humanity, his work also reflected the racist ideas of the pseudoscientists who came before him, going back some 200 years.

Based on the tenets of biology, geology, botany, and so on, Darwin's work brought clarity to the early formulation of evolution, concretized it, and claimed that there would come a time when the gap between human and ape would increase by the anticipated extinction of intermediates such as the chimpanzee and "Hottentot" (Gould, 1981). In other words, Darwin considered the Hottentot, a derogatory name that refers to the Khoisan people of South Africa, the link between ape and human that would eventually disappear through the human evolutionary process. We shall see that Darwin was not the first to believe in African intermediaries between apes and humans.

Of course, Europe had been set up to establish this race idea by those whose work influenced Darwin. William Petty wrote *Of the Scale of Creatures* in 1676, in which he asserted his belief that Europeans were superior to African people in color, behavior, and mentality and constituted a separate species (Lindqvist, 1992/2007). William Tyson viewed the small African people, labeled by Europeans as "Pygmies," in his 1708 work *The Anatomy of a Pigmy* as animals, "wholly brutes," closer to primates than other humans. In this biological construct, the small African woman, man, and child were considered the intermediary between ape and man. Georges Cuvier's (1769–1832) studies showed that species vanished, possibly through catastrophic environmental changes, and that it was likely that this would happen to the new ones. His 1816 book *The Animal Kingdom* divided humanity into three races, stating that the "Negroid races" bore similarities to primates and remained in a state of barbarism. Greatly influenced by Cuvier's idea of the role of environmental changes, Europeans applied Cuvier's thinking to human beings. Those who could adapt would survive. Robert Knox (1791–1862) also believed in the special place of Europeans and wrote the book *The Races of Man: A Fragment* (1850/2014) as an explicit guide to Europeans about their superior position. Knox was a Scottish anatomist who spent the latter part of his life studying and writing about evolutionary theory.

In Knox's theories, the darker races were inferior to the white races. He claims that while studying the corpse of a "colored" man he observed that the colored man had a third fewer nerves in his legs and arms than the white and therefore must be a third less in terms of soul, instinct, and reason. On the basis of examining one darker person, Knox concluded an entire gallery of opinions about human beings. He admits in this book that he does not know the origin of humans, and this is a good indication of the nonsense that would then be uttered by this man of science from the University of Edinburgh. For him, human beings seem coeval with the rest of nature. Of course, now we know that the earth is nearly 5 billion years old and *Homo sapiens* are only about 300,000 years old There is no way that humans were on earth at the beginning of time. Despite his factual error, and there was perhaps no way for him to know the age of the earth in his time, it is his errors in judgment about human beings that are most distasteful, because his silly notions about human beings are at the beginning of the British contributions to the minimizing of humans from other parts of the world. In fact, we claim that Knox, along with the other unscientific Europeans who pontificated about the nature of humanity, as purveyors of the madness that led to the genocide of the indigenous people of North America, Australia, and Tasmania and the attempted murder of all the people of South America, Asia, and Africa, was operating on the basis of this false idea.

By 1871, Darwin had transferred nature's struggle for existence onto humans and defined the concept of evolution, to account for a natural order in that those who survived were the improved, approved version of humans. Lindqvist draws a link between these beliefs and the development of the gun as the tool of conquest. We go further to assert that in all cases the enslavement of African women, men, and children was not only a full onslaught, but the enslavement of African people could also be viewed as religiously determined, thus providing the justification of the wholesale debasement, enslavement, and murder of African people.

These ideas continued with writers such as Kant, Buffon, Hegel, Jefferson, and Voltaire. Blumenbach's classification scheme favored a European conception of humans as the standard. Thus, he gave the nomenclature for what he considered the "most perfect skull," the term "Caucasian," derived from the belief that the most perfect skull had been found in the Caucasus mountains of southern Russia. Clearly, Blumenbach's claim that this skull was "perfect" was purely personal, but it gained acceptance in Europe; but alas, Caucasoid skulls were found on all continents. There was nothing that could be called a perfect skull if it were human, yet this was taught in the Pan-European Academy. It is a falsehood that is a fundamental tenet of race and racism, and it exists as the subtext of all European academic disciplines taught across the world and is a critical feature of the "Pan-European Academy," a term invented by Chinweizu, which refers to the control of Europe on its implantation of academia and academicians across its colonized world.

To succeed in the academy, one is taught the theoretical disciplines and principles that will maintain the race hierarchy, and black and "red" academics who pursue ways to use these disciplines to bring to the fore the reality of the conditions of life and death faced by those of lower ranking in the hierarchy of humanity are dismissed. Black and red women, men, and children are examples of those most disenfranchised as indigenous and African people, respectively, in the Americas, North, South, and Central. Russell Thornton's (1987) important work *American Indian Holocaust and Survival* addresses holocaust as a long-term enterprise of genocide initiated by contact with the Europeans in 1492 that took on many guises until the current time. In the process of the loss of roughly 68 million red women, men, and children in the Americas, Thornton includes these determinants: warfare, genocide, disease, land removal from sacred lands, destruction of ways of life, fertility declines, slave hunters, Christianity, wars among First Nations people initiated by the European conquerors, as well as population growth among the conquerors. Viewing holocaust from this perspective provides a basis for understanding its continuity as well as other holocausts, such as the continuing African one, which has been ignored in much the same way as that of the First Nations (black) people of Australia, who by our definition of humanity are part of the same holocaust. Marimba Ani (1989) introduced *Maafa*, a Kiswahili term meaning "disaster," in her book *Let the Circle be Unbroken*. *Maafa* is used to include the nature of the ongoing African holocaust, including the suppression of cultural beliefs, values, and spirituality, from the Arabic conquest of Africa until the current times. We may look outside the race construct and see that what we have been experiencing is in reality a clash of cultures.

In the face of this continuing cultural reality, we ask whether black academicians living in and practicing non-African and African cultures that have enslaved and colonized and murdered black bodies, minds, and souls can shed the cultural constraints of race as an authentic identity and understand the development of cultural identity as the basis of more progressive ideas regarding humanity. As Diop theorized, it is possible to reconnect to African beliefs and values that are a historical part of our cultural and ancestral memory. Cultural collective memory can be reawakened in the new light of discovery through our Afrocentric episteme regarding questions of who we are, why we are here, how we got here, and where we shall go.

Returning to a history of African decline from preconquest times to now, David Brion Davis's *Slavery and Human Progress* (1966) highlights some of the contradictions that arise in how enslavers viewed African enslavement as a form of human progress, especially regarding the development of technology, economic growth, standard of living, and so on. From an Afrocentric perspective, one wonders how human progress can be associated with human degradation. This perspective is only possible if some humans, namely black and red humanity, are viewed as less than human or subhuman, whose lives are expendable. According to Davis,

Prince Henry of Portugal, who reviewed the first shipment of enslaved African people brought to Europe in the 1440s, thought of the salvation of those lost, reflecting on those who need never experience the horrors of enslavement. Davis notes the spread of enslavement from the Mediterranean to the Caribbean and Brazil and the competition between Europeans and the Islamic world. Plantation enslavement was not,

> invented by lawless buccaneers and New World adventurers as nineteenth century liberals often charged but was a creation of the most progressive peoples and forces in Europe—Italian merchants; Iberian explorers; Jewish inventors, traders and cartographers; Dutch, German and British investors and bankers.... Black slavery was an intrinsic part of the "rise of the west." (pp. xvi–xvii)

Here, we see how liberal minds are in fact racist minds and what they all have in common are their cultural beliefs and values, which bond them in the recognition of a perceived, yet contrived, inferiority of African humanity (Fanon, 2008). Moreover, they embrace the satisfaction of "knowing" that their cultural group, which has transitioned from patriarchy to white supremacy as white women have conspired with white men, claims a higher position in the racial hierarchy of humanity, from which they benefit. This important point will help us understand not only how racism evolved as an agreement between patriarchal women and men but also how white supremacist women, who give birth to the new rising supremacists, cannot, in reality, be separated from their men in a cultural enterprise from which they both benefit. We view the construction of race as endorsed by patriarchy and the major oppression that African/black women, men, and children face as one coin with two sides.

In the effort to own and control the world's resources, Europeans enslaved African women, men, and children and brutally denied their humanity. Karl Marx cogently defined, analyzed, and articulated this merciless, inhuman process of accumulating wealth as capitalism. As suggested earlier, the psychological and behavioral characteristics of patriarchy may be viewed as superiority, slothfulness, indolence, individualism, greed, aggression, and, we may add, inhumanity, which refers to one's uncivilized behavior, the fundamental requirement of European capitalism that underpinned the so-called development of the Western Industrial Revolution. In highlighting the miserable, unconscionable state of the working European poor, Marx failed to give equal value to the humanity of the enslaved African people. By defining African enslavement "slavery" as primitive accumulation, a lower stage in human and economic development than capitalist accumulation, a higher stage in economic and human development, Marx marginalized and minimalized the lives and energies of African people, which were so critical to that process (Dove, 1995). Evolution provides a fundamental tenet in European history, from which it is loosely and basically understood that human life began in Africa through transforming from monkeys to humans, changing from ignorant barbarians into the modern "civilized" persons of today. European epistemology is grounded in the so-called knowledge that humans go through developmental stages toward civilization—which include (not necessarily in this order) the hunter-gatherer, a lower stage; spirituality and ancestral respect, a lower stage; matriarchy, a lower stage; enslavement, a lower stage; monotheistic religiosity, a higher stage; urbanity, a higher stage; and materiality and profit, a higher stage. The belief is that less melaninated people are advanced in human evolution as a higher stage of human development. Essentially, this evolutionist, melaninist concept was fundamental to the construction of race and the justification of white supremacy.

Contrary to such ideas and according to Edward Bruce Bynum (2012), melanin in reality is significant to all life in that it exists in all humans. One is unable to live without it. It is in the brain and all the vital organs, in the spinal cord and eyes, assisting with sight. Melanin stores and conducts light, which exists as energy in humans, in the atmosphere, as well as in the outer layers of the planet Earth. It is viewed as a vibrational feature in awakening the mind and consciousness.

> Melanin and neuromelanin reach their zenith of concentration and activity in the brain and nervous system of our own species, regardless of the surface or purported racial differentiation. The biological significance of surface or mere skin racial typing within the human species is presently a minor scientific fact but a politically painful dynamic. From the global human perspective, it is a phenotypic permutation of small consequence in the ocean of genetic and biological similarity. However, deeper down we share this subtle bioluminescence and bioelectrical aspect of our nervous systems. Our brains and internal organ systems, regardless of ethnicity are covered with light-sensitive melanin.... We share a residence and resonance with each other in this cosmos of light and living darkness. (p. 10)

In this dark–light, it is all the more astonishing—perhaps insane is a more appropriate description—that melanin and its amazing properties would be a way to consider, advance, and assert a level of superiority over those who have more melanin in their skins, when we all need it to exist and are in fact biologically the same. As Diop theorized, it is culture that creates the major differences among us, and they are based either on female–male reciprocity or a male–female hierarchy, domination.

Southwest Asian Culture and Race

According to Ben-Levi (1986) the term *Hebrew ibr* is a verb used by the ancient Canaanites meaning "to pass" or "to cross over" and is first recorded in Genesis 14:13 as a slang term *Ha-Ibri* to identify Abraham, the father of the Hebrew religion, as "the one who crossed over" the Euphrates River to the land of Canaan. The Tanakh is a collection of Old Testament Hebraic teachings, the first five books of the Bible, from which the belief in Christianity has evolved. It supplies the notion of the races of humanity in Genesis in the story of the three sons of Noah, Ham, Japheth, and Shem, peopling the world after the Great Deluge. Essentially, Ham would father the black people, Hamites; Shem, the "mixed-race" Semites; and Japheth, the Aryans or whites. The hierarchical notion of their father's favoritism is mirrored in the supposed beginning and future history of the world's people. In the story, Ham witnessed his father Noah in a nude and inebriated state and did not cover him, whereas his brothers did. It is said that Noah then cursed his son Ham by condemning Ham's fourth son Canaan and all descendants of Canaan to a life of servitude to his uncles, Shem and Japheth.

An early version of Noah's story is recorded in the 6th century Babylonian Talmud, which evolved from 100 BCE and was a part of the Tanakh, prior to the coming of Muhammed and Islam in the 7th century. In this story, Noah's son Ham saw his father sleeping naked in the night and castrated him for no apparent or stated reason. When Noah awoke, he cursed his son Ham, telling him that as a result of his not being able to have a fourth son, Ham's fourth son, Canaan, would have children ugly because of the crime, black because of the night when it happened, with twisted hair for turning to see his nakedness with red eyes, with swollen lips for making fun of his father; and with long penises because he was naked. These offspring would be called "Negroes" (Poe, 1997). The word for that time was most likely similar to *abd*, an Arabic word used to indicate "black" or "slave" and used interchangeably to describe the obscene, a person lacking moral stature or a filthy person, a person practicing a non-Muslim religion, or the Nuba of South Sudan, who were historically enslaved (Jok, 2001).

There are varying stories about what Ham did when he saw his father. Influenced by the Abrahamic tradition, the Arab/Muslim/Shem version is that black people are cursed to be slaves and menials, Semites are blessed to be prophets and nobles, while whites are destined to be kings and tyrants (Lewis, 1990)

The preoccupation with the castration of Noah by Ham is important as castration has been and continues to be a significant punishment for the African man, alive or dead. One can see from Ham's so-called castration of his father in this make-believe story propounded as truth that this action justified the castration of African men captured and enslaved by Semitic people, although in the Arab/Semitic world this cruel punishment has been viewed rather as a privilege bestowed. Of the hundreds of millions of African women and men enslaved by Semites of Abrahamic, Muslim, Christian, or other religious persuasions, countless African men were castrated. According to Azumah (2001), during the 1700s, many of these enslaved African men were used as eunuchs, forming a special class of black men who would be entrusted with the charge to guard harems, the wives of high-ranking men, and serve as attendants at holy sites. Castration was literally the only way African men could attain a high position of any kind within the Muslim world outside black Africa. Of the African boys castrated, only a small percentage survived.

One wonders whether the enslaved African men and women were able to have children and families in these abhorrent conditions; in fact, as Lewis (1990) asserts, there was only a small increase in the number of enslaved African women and men. He lists these causes:

- Many enslaved men were imported as eunuchs and thus precluded from having offspring. Among these were many who otherwise by the wealth and power that they acquired might have founded families.
- Another group of enslaved men who rose to positions of great power were the military, who were normally liberated at some stage in their career and their offspring given freedom.
- Those enslaved as menial, domestic, and manual workers remained in the conditions of servitude and transmitted that condition to their descendants. There were not many descendants as "mating" was not permitted and marriage was not encouraged.

- There was a high death toll among all classes of enslaved African women, men, and children, from military commanders to menials. African people lacked immunity to diseases. They died in large numbers from endemic diseases as well as epidemics. As late as the 19th century, Western travelers in North Africa and Egypt noted the high death rate among the enslaved African people.

Using the research of Thornton (1987) regarding the process of genocide of his people, we apply it to African people's experiences. Genocide takes place through

- warfare;
- "slave" hunters—enslavers;
- land and mineral wealth acquisition;
- its justification by Christian and Islamic anti-black/African beliefs;
- land removal from sacred lands;
- destruction of ways of life and imposition of alien cultural forms;
- internal wars initiated by the conquerors;
- population growth among the conquerors;
- vulnerability to unfamiliar diseases;
- impoverishment and degradation;
- murders, individual or state initiated; and
- depression and suicide.

These experiences all lead to fertility decline.

Castration in North America was viewed as a punishment for African enslaved men for more than 250 years. Cress Welsing's (1991) psychological analysis of white supremacy notes that many African men lynched by white men had their genitals removed by them. They kept them as trophies. Welsing views castration as indicating the white supremacist's envy and fear of the African's penis and its genetic potential. This envy can be understood within the race paradigm going back more than 2,000 years as a very real threat to maintaining the race hierarchy. Ironically, the Southwest Asian belief in castration for the African man was to prevent procreation, but in the situation of the African man in America, procreation was critical for the production of enslaved children to create profit; thus in death, castration fulfilled the desire for white supremacists to take their trophy.

Today, the practice continues as African men are castrated during the buying and selling of enslaved African people in places like Libya and Saudi Arabia (Atlanta Black Star, 2017). Historically, eunuchs, offering no threat of fathering children, often looked after the wives or concubines of wealthy slavers, and some rose to high positions in the society. The ability to rise to a privileged position has enabled some, even to this day, to believe that this elite status demonstrates that there is no racism in Arabo-Islamic cultural beliefs, much like the U.S. situation, where a black president is said to indicate that racism does not, has not, and will not exist.

As recently as 1995, findings from the research by Philippe Rushton (1997) involving penis size as a measure of intelligence indicated that black men had the largest penises and were the least intelligent, yellow men were the most intelligent with the tiniest penises, and white men had neither large nor small penises. Interestingly, Rushton's book was published by the Charles Darwin Research Institute and is in its third print.

The focus on men is not to ignore the heinous treatment of enslaved African women. In Islam, those women considered most desirable were used as sexual objects, concubines, and wives and whatever their Semitic enslavers desired, not to speak of the cruel treatment of those women considered to be "ugly," very likely because of their darker hue. The identity of Zanj is a negative reference to African people enslaved by Arabs. Whether the root of this word is African, Arabic, or Persian has not been clarified. According to Marina Tolmacheva (1986), it may be an ethnic word for a particular African nation, it may relate to the color black, or it may be a negative term referring to non-Islamic African people; it has been associated with cannibalism and barbarity and used as a term to define a collective group of enslaved African women, men, and children who may come from different parts of Africa, not necessarily on the northeastern or eastern coast. What we do understand is that based on Arabo-Semitic religiosity, which includes the debasement and demonization of the African, it is used as a negative term to refer to dark-skinned enslaved African women and men in today's Sudan. The Zanj uprising in the 9th century would not have endeared these African people to their enslavers, as they fought for their freedom many times, culminating in a war in Baghdad that lasted 15 years (868–883 CE). It is considered the first major organized fight against the enslavers, well before the Haitian Revolution (1791–1804). Ironically, the so-called Zanj woman was useful to breastfeed the enslavers' children and care for them, although her character was deemed untrustworthy and there was no pleasure to be got from her because of her stench and the coarseness of her body (Azumah, 2001). She was deemed to be fit for rape, which meant that in essence she could not be raped as there was no such crime; this can be likened to the same beliefs attached to the Dalit women of India through Brahminism and, ultimately, black women across the world. In the current conditions of the enslaved Dinka women of Sudan, sexual exploitation is an important part of her abuse, whereby she may be forced to have sex at any given time, not only with master but also with his sons, to prevent them from becoming homosexual (Jok, 2001).

What is so abhorrent is that these Sudanese women, now considered beneath the feet of their enslavers, are the descendants of the famous Kushite women—mothers, queens, leaders, priestesses, farmers, scientists, mathematicians, musicians, and so on, who along with their kings, fathers, brothers, husbands, sons, and so on, founded Kemet and African matriarchy thousands of years ago. Meroe and Napata are two remaining sites of governance in the disappearing lands once known as Kush that exist inside today's Sudan. To Hebraic practitioners, Kush, the name of one of the sons of Ham, who castrated his father, Noah, refers to the lands of Africans or black people. To the Arabs, Sudan, an amalgamation of ancient nations inhabiting the area of Kush, means the land of slaves.

Given the popularity of African male castration, it is conceivable that the castration of the tip of the woman's clitoris is related. Perhaps like the castrated man, she was more prized (as she would have less or no sexual feeling) and would "behave" appropriately in the company of the men belonging to enslaver women. As Hunwick (1985) believes, it is ironical that the way to life for an African woman was her sexuality whereas for the man, it was the sacrifice of his sexuality (Azumah, 2001).

When trying to link this fear of the African phallus, one may conceivably relate this to the ancient African divinity Min, referenced in the pyramid texts, whose temple at Gebtu is evidence of a priest and possibly a priestess following; thus, the dating of his influence cannot be known at this time. His image is located at the tomb of a princess in Giza (Hart, 2002). The image of the divinity Min stood with an erect penis, symbolizing regeneration, reproduction, sexuality, and procreation, the symbolism of which very likely extended to nature and life, much like the principles of Asar (Osiris, the husband of Aset, Isis), who later, without the penis, represented reproduction, rebirth, resurrection, nature, and vegetation. It may well be that Min's existence is referenced in the Rig Veda, the Brahmin holy text, when during the conquest of the Kushites in India, the Indo-Aryans noted disparagingly that they whom they called *Dasa* were matriarchal and "worshippers of the phallus" (Chandler, 1988).

Indo-European Culture and Race

Evidence of racist beliefs and practices are revealed in India in Brahmanism, the Hindu religion, which is based on ideas of reincarnation. Brahmanism was created by the conquering Indo-Europeans (Aryans) and codified in the Rig Veda around 1000 BCE (Jackson, 1937/2015). The Aryans arrived in the Indus Valley around 1800 BCE. The black indigenous Kushites of the Indus Valley complex, known as the builders of the Harappan civilization, were a matriarchal, literate people who had existed and flourished for well over 1,000 years before the Aryans conquered and destroyed their civilization (Ben-Levi, 1986; Chandler, 1988; Fairservis, 1988; Rajshekar, 1987; Rashidi & Van Sertima, 1988; Stone, 1976). Led by their war god Indra, the Aryans slaughtered the Kushite women, men, and children, whom they called *Dasa*, described in the Brahman scripture as dark and ill-favored, bull-lipped, snub-nosed worshippers of the phallus (Chandler, 1988). The scripture also states that the mind of the woman brooks no discipline. Her intellect has little weight (Stone, 1976).

The Rig Veda defines four castes or races (*varnas*) by five statuses identified by the colors white, red, yellow, and black. White was associated with the Brahmins, the teachers and priests; red with the Kshatriyas, the warriors; yellow with the Vaisyas, the merchants and farmers; and black with the Sudras, the lowest *varna*. The Sudras were considered to be born as sinners, were easily identifiable by their skin color, and had no right to listen to the "holy" words or become literate to read them. Below the Sudras were the Dalits, born outside the four castes as "untouchables" and debased in life; thus, their lives had to be lived in servility, humiliation, and degradation. The untouchables comprised "unholy" alliances between the races and the indigenous people, whose ancestors had fought the Aryans. They were outcasts enslaved by the religious regime. To facilitate continuing separation of the races, the Laws of Manu—a devious set of rules devised by Manu, a fictitious sage—were employed by the dominating group, the Brahmins. Marriage was forbidden between the superior races and the inferior ones, with dire consequences for disobedience: A man who married a Sudra woman became an outcast; a Brahman who married a Sudra woman would essentially rot in hell after death. If a low-caste man in arrogance spits, urinates, or breaks wind against a superior, his lips, penis, or anus (respectively) would be cut off (Rashidi &

Van Sertima, 1988). The Sudra (man) had the opportunity to rise if he was pure, the servant of betters, gentle in speech, and free from pride, and if he sought refuge within Brahminism (Rashidi & Van Sertima, 1988). In other words, if the Sudra man accepted his unjust, inferior human status, regardless of the treatment, and bore this humiliation without challenging it, then he would have the possibility of returning as a higher race in his next incarnation. In comparison, it is interesting that the African man in Arabia may rise to an elite status if he has been castrated and behaves well, and that castration is considered a high honor.

By placing the Dalits as a race outside religion, Brahmanism created a hierarchy within the black race (as they saw it) where superiority was determined by the practice of the religion and, thus, the perceived alliance with the rulers. Yet both Sudras and Dalits were despised and abused by the "superior" races and damned in their scriptures, based entirely on their blackness.

In Dr. Babasaheb Ambedkar's famous discourse "The Annihilation of Caste" (1936/2016), his undelivered speech to the annual conference for the Jat-Pat-Todak Mandal of Lahore, Part II, he refers to the treatment of Dalits in Poona, the capital of the Peshwas, where untouchables carried a broom around their waists to sweep away the dust that they had stepped on so as not to pollute the earth in case a Hindu was to tread on the same ground. Around the neck of a Dalit hung a pot that would hold the spit if any should fall so that it did not pollute the earth where the Hindu would tread. In Zanu in Ahmedabad District of Gujarat, untouchable women working for the wealthy began to carry water in metal pots instead of earthenware pots; it was considered an affront to Hindus for an untouchable to use a higher-status pot. The women were assaulted for their crime. Dr Ambedkar further elucidates on the Balais, a community of untouchables. They were forbidden to wear anything that was above their status; they had to be at the beck and call of Hindus and accept for their services whatever was given. The Balais could not allow their cattle to graze on

Hindu lands if passing through. Conversely, Hindus did not allow their cattle to graze in the fields of the Balais. The children were not allowed to attend government-run schools, and the injustices remained generation after generation. If the Balais did not abide by these rules, they had to leave their homes in their villages. More recently in August 2014, a report was released in the New York City–based Human Rights Watch that detailed the practice of "manual scavenging"—the collecting of excrement from latrines by hand. The job is done by the Dalits, or untouchables, who often face threats of violence, eviction and withheld wages if they attempt to escape this disgusting burden. Women collect human feces from private homes and carry it in baskets that spill over them, reifying their status as untouchables.

In light of such realities, one asks, how did Mohandas Karamchand Gandhi, the most famous Brahmin, reconcile being a member of, and a participant in, a spiritual system that purposely debases those of the lower orders, Dalits, who were forbidden to even caste their eyes on a person of higher status? The predicament is that Dalits, who are supposedly not good enough for the religion, are tied to the religion and in this way are justifiably enslaved and debased through the religion. Ironically, it was not Gandhi but Dr Ambedkar who, himself a Dalit, was the most famous activist who fought for the dismantling of this heinous construct. Dr Ambedkar tried to gain the support of Gandhi to annihilate this abhorrent belief system. Of Gandhi, Dr Ambedkar (1936/2016) said, "To many a Hindu he is an oracle, so great that when he opens his lips it is expected that the argument must close, and no dog must bark" (from the preface to the second edition). However, Gandhi never did support Dr Ambedkar, who correctly thought that race did not exist; but caste he believed was an imposed construction that created a distance among groups of humans that would follow their descendants forever, for no logical reason. While Dr Ambedkar has demolished the notion of race as not true, our position is that based on the ancient construction of Brahminism, its origins are grounded in the concept of race, which informs the caste divisions. Untouchability is an amalgamation of forbidden relationships between castes, and as such, there may be lighter-skinned untouchables. This does not refute the melanin-based distinctions. Very likely the lightness of Dr Ambedkar's skin color enabled him the privilege to become "educated" and speak on behalf of untouchables. This also happens in the African American situation, where there are light-skinned people, like W. E. B. Du Bois, Malcolm X, Angela Davis, Melina Abdullah, and Colin Kaepernick, who have stood up to speak against the injustices imposed on people of African descent, including the most melaninated.

Furthermore, while race is untrue, most of the world views it as a scientific and/or religious fact. This is why we are writing about the cultural construction of race. We see race in the same light as and use "race" to define any system of hierarchy in which color is a predominant factor that defines the status of humanity to their descendants. We have tried to show that the belief in race has determined the maltreatment and deaths of millions of the darkest-skinned women, men, and children across the world, who ironically are the ancestors of humanity.

Owing to these beliefs, black-skinned African women, men, and children are being enslaved, tortured, abused, and killed in these societies even to this day. We can surmise that these racist beliefs were being enacted prior to their codification in the Abrahamic/Babylonian Talmud from 100 BCE to 500–600 CE, the Rig Veda of Hinduism/Brahmanism at around 1000 BCE, the Christian Bible at around 100 CE, and the Quran at around 700 CE.

Race in Northern Africa

In 1971, Lewis, a British American historian, published *Race and Color in Islam*, with the precise purpose of exposing the roots and representations of color in the Islamic tradition. Reading Lewis's book, one is struck by the commonplace uses of "black" in a negative sense among the Arabs and others in the Islamic tradition. In effect, the religion dictates the attitudes found in the society prior to the establishment of Islam, which means that the origin of the nasty memes of race and color predated the Muslims. They are inheritors of the negativities surrounding blackness. When Lewis expanded his work in 1990, he gave the work the name *Race and Slavery in the Middle East: An Historical Enquiry*. Lewis seemed to have understood much more about the relationship of Islam to complexion than some other writers. In fact, the history of northern Africa is filled with the conquest of the indigenous black populations by the Islamic jihadists who stormed out of Arabia in the 7th century with the message of Prophet Muhammad and dominated African lands from Egypt to Mauritania in the next 2 centuries. The converts to Islam became some of the fiercest warriors for the Saracen armies that invaded southern Europe. Thus, the Islamized Africans were referred to as Moors. This name distinguished the converts from the Saracens or Arabs, both names for the desert dwellers who emerged as a powerful force in the 7th century.

In his second book on this subject, *Race and Slavery in the Middle East*, Lewis (1990) also shows that he understood the relationship between enslavement and color. Slavery is a system of permanent bondage maintained by violence and domination of all aspects of a person's life by someone who has managed to gain physical power over the captives. The Arabs, like the Europeans who would come after them in the invading of Africa, held the belief that blackness was negative. Indeed, we see in writers such as Edward Said (2003) in *Orientalism* and also in Lewis's books a capture by the racial classification that has been ossified in historical writing. For example, Said's *Orientalism* is essentially an Arab claim on the ancient Egyptian inheritance that ignores the African history of Egypt. At one time, the Orient meant China and perhaps India, but to claim Egypt for the Orient is to introduce confusion into history. It is no wonder that the University of Pennsylvania Museum separated Ancient

Egypt from the rest of Africa or that the University of Chicago organized Egypt as part of Oriental Studies rather than African Studies; one finds similar constructions in London and in Paris as well. As important as Lewis is to this discourse, he too is captured by the racial doctrine elevated by white supremacists. Lewis (1990) writes, "The ancient Egyptians were closely acquainted with their black southern neighbors and sometimes portray them, in words or pictures, with characteristic Negroid features" (p. 17). In the following passage, he refers to the often cited event of Peraa Senursert III, in the 19th century BCE, supposedly restricting the access of blacks to Egyptian territory. But this is a racist interpretation where no race existed; in the racial sense, one could say that the two people were of the same African race. Making the issue one of Negroes or blacks being barred from entry into Egypt is literally odd. There were no people designated as "Negro" during the 19th century BCE. This is a terrible misuse of the Kemetic word *Nehusi* or *Nehesi*, which refers to the Nubian people, who were physically not different from the Kemetic people, the *Remetiu*. To translate *Nehesi* as "Negro" is to misconstrue the language and to infiltrate into Egyptian history the problems of contemporary Western culture. One could not or would not say that the Scots closed their borders to bar the Caucasians from the south; they are both Caucasian in contemporary racial usage. The same holds true for Remitiu, Egyptians, Kemetic people, and Nehesi, Nubians, and Kushites, who lived south of them. They are merely different nations.

The Saracens or Arabs knew they were not indigenous to northern Africa but descendants of the desert people of Arabia or the Sinai Peninsula. "Saracen" is the word often used by Latin and Greek writers to refer to desert dwellers. However, the presence of the language of Arabia is first attested to in the mid-9th century BCE. Before this time, there is no mention in any text of the Arabic language or people per se. In the Hebrew language, the word *Arvi* came to be used for "Arab," meaning "desert dweller." Arabic is not a language indigenous to Egypt; the ancient Egyptians spoke ciKam, the language of Kemet, often referred to in texts as *Mdw Ntr*, divine words. Indeed, this is important to understand the subsequent discussion about Ancient Egypt, which gets darker and blacker the farther back in history one goes. Arabs, descendants of the Bedouins, came into Egypt at the request of the black population to assist in expelling the Romans who had occupied the land since the death of Cleopatra. When General El As, the leader of the Arab Islamic army that had defeated Jerusalem, entered Egypt, he liked what he saw of the country and began the construction of his capital city, Cairo, in 639 CE. It was from this fortressed city that the Saracen-Arabs began their conquest of northern Africa, bringing many black nations, including Tamashek, Amazigh, Fulani, Hausa, Peul, and Toubou, under their religious and military control. This control of the northern part of the continent with the converted African armies of Moors as their hammer was the beginning of the confusion that led to the quaint and odd arguments about the nature of Ancient Egypt.

With the preceding information in hand, it is now easy to see how Western writers became embroiled in racist discourses about Ancient Kemet, the black nation. Egypt is the Greek name for the country that Africans called Kemet. Homer, the first Greek who wrote something that was considered important, lived around 800 BCE; however, the black people of Egypt had completed most of the pyramids by 2500 BCE! Prior to Homer's writings, there is no mention of the name "Egypt." The ancient writings of the land speak of Kemet, the black nation or the land of black people. Now we see that the changing of the name of the nation to Egypt was an intrusion into the psycho-space of African people and served as the base for the race paradigm to inflict its damage on future thinkers. Aegyptos, the houses of Ptah, was not what the people called the Two Lands, the Beloved Land; once again, we emphasize that they referred to it as "Kemet."

Cheikh Anta Diop (1974) wrote, "Ancient Egypt was a Negro civilization. The history of black Africa will remain suspended in air and cannot be written correctly until African historians dare to connect it with the history of Egypt" (p. xiv). Much of Diop's thinking was influenced by Herodotus and other ancient Greek writers but also by Count Volney, a French explorer who was called Constantin François de Chassebœuf. Volney wrote *Les Ruines, ou méditations sur les revolutions des empires* (1791/1950), which in English is often shortened to *Ruins of Empire*. Volney's essay on the philosophy of history included a prediction that there would be a union of all religions when people see that they have a common underlying theme. However, he advanced the thought that Africans had been pushed to the side by those who had little understanding of history. And he wondered,

> How is it that a people now forgotten discovered, while others were yet barbarians, the elements of the arts and the sciences? A race now rejected from society for their sable skin and frizzled hair founded on the study of the laws of nature those civil and religious systems which still govern the universe. (p. 2)

Volney's use of the word "sable" is deliberate because he meant to state from his observations during his travels for seven months in Egypt that even with the Arab overlords of Egypt ruling since the 7th century CE there was still evidence of the blackness of the ancient Egyptians in the culture and manner and physical presence of the masses of people. The word "sable" was often used in European heraldry to mean the blackest of black tinctures. Volney sought to use neither the word "brown" nor the term "light brown" in his description of those who basically brought civilization through the sciences and arts.

Volney's book was published before Champollion succeeded in deciphering the language of Kemet in 1822. Once the language was deciphered, the immensity of Kemet's civilization began to unfold in massive chapters of knowledge, like one was seeing a documentary of the history of literature, geometry, biology, philosophy, astronomy, and medicine, among other arts and sciences. Embedded in this powerful discovery of the genius of the builders of the classical African traditions along the Nile River was the seed of Eurocentric rebellion against the African people. How could Africans have built the pyramids? Perhaps the writings of the 5th century historian Herodotus were incorrect, they questioned. How could "black" people have built the first majestic civilizations of antiquity?

These questions get to the point of our thesis that the racial ladder, with its descriptive statements about African people, black people, being lazy, childlike, inferior in character and physical characteristics, simple-minded, and similar to animals, prevents the expression of humanity and cripples the imagination of European writers who cannot believe that the people they have been taught to hate and despise were the creators of Kemet and Nubia. In their minds, if Europeans or Asians did not enter Africa and build these civilizations, then the builders must have been "aliens" from other planets! Until Europeans are able to reconcile themselves to the fact that all *Homo sapiens* derived from an African woman who lived nearly 300,000 years ago, they will not be able to see that Ancient Kemet was a black country. The task will be difficult because the racist memes have continued for so long in the West that the so-called white people have been victimized by their racist imaginations. It is a public health crisis among European populations, who are now being confronted by humans in every region asking questions about their primitive beliefs that only Europeans are intelligent, rational, and wise.

So here are some of the facts that we know. Writing appeared in Kemet about 3500 BCE. The first human to unite many kingdoms into one state was Menes, an African from the interior of the continent, who conquered 42 kingdoms to make Kemet the world's first united states. Nearly 1,000 years after Menes, the African philosopher, physician, and geometer Imhotep built the first pyramid, the Sakkara Pyramid, for King Zoser.

We have traveled throughout Kemet, looking past its Christian and Islamic history to its original, African moral and ethical ideas to understand the meaning of the ancient culture. It was African in every sense, and that is why we call it classical Africa. What the ancient Africans of the Nile Valley developed were prototypes of many of the cultural products, icons, and contributions that we see in other parts of the continent. Classical civilizations exist because they have the capacity to inspire other nations and societies. Ma'at, for example, is the first spiritual idea in the ancient world, predating anything in Europe, Asia, or the Americas. It is fundamentally about unity, truth, justice, righteousness, order, harmony, balance, and reciprocity. These are the wellsprings for other African societies.

We know from the paintings on the tombs and temples that the creators of this civilization were the black people of the Nile Valley. They painted themselves, and the Europeans who saw the paintings were often at a loss for words. First, they said that Egypt was not in Africa, and of course, the map proves this to be false. Some said that Egypt is in Africa but the Egyptians came from outside Africa. This could never be shown because the Nile River runs from the south toward the north and the Mediterranean civilizations came from the Sudan, Uganda, and Ethiopia and down the river to Kemet. Some Europeans reluctantly admitted that Egyptians built the civilization but the ancient Egyptians were not blacks but "reddish-brown" people. Authors who wrote like this quickly lost historical face because the only reddish-brown people are the people of Africa. Of course, there is a variety of blackness on the walls of the tombs; that is to be expected since blackness is not necessarily uniform, even today.

It is not our intention to delve deeply into this discourse but rather to dispense with this issue by saying that melanin studies have proved that the ancient Egyptians were black skinned. Ancient Greek writers have said that they had "wooly hair" and "black skin," as in the Greek word *melanchroes*. Good common sense shows us that the ancient Egyptians lived next to some of the blackest-complexioned people on the globe, the people of Sudan, and when the Egyptians in ancient times depicted themselves and the Nubians of today's Sudan, they were the same complexion, black. Hence, the proximity of Kemet to Nubia, as with Scotland and England, shows the similarities between them; this is not some "racial" difference, just national identities based on family ancestors. One can travel to contemporary to Upper Egypt, the south, and still see the remnants of the ancient people, who have not been thoroughly mixed with all of the invaders who occupied Egypt, as we see in the northern part of the country.

Our aim in this chapter was to demonstrate how the racial paradigm found its way into the interpretation of Africa's classical civilizations, often cutting off discussions by Africans themselves of the interconnectivity of the African culture. With the destruction of the racial ladder, so that we all become human, we will see an explosion of human will to bring into existence some of the common vision that Volney predicted. Of course, we will have to accept African primacy in terms of humanity and human civilization so that we can then start from the fact of our common heritage, ecological ethics, totemic protection of animals and plants, unity of all humans, and the moral acceptance of Ma'at regardless of class or language.

This brings us to a discussion about the use of color in the ancient Egyptian tradition, which alongside Nubia represents the classical traditions of Africa. While there has been contestation by Westerners and some Asians against the idea of the blackness of ancient Egyptians, the evidence of the blackness of the Africans of Egypt is indisputable. It is only out of the race paradigm that this issue can be questioned. In other words, the race paradigm suggests that "black" means backward, lazy, unintelligent, indolent, emotional, and ugly. Thus, those who questioned the color of the ancient Egyptians are perplexed by the brilliance of a society that was created only in Africa by black people. The argument, using the race paradigm, has to be that this is impossible given the negativity associated with blackness as a color.

Hence, there has been throughout the history of Western discourse about ancient Egypt a consistent attempt to refute Egypt's blackness, to the dismay of rational thinkers and African historians. Of course, Diop, the late Senegalese scientist, battled against Western and Arab scholars in his books *The African Origin of Civilization* (1974) and *Civilization or Barbarism: An Authentic Anthropology* (1992). In 1973, Diop was invited to an international conference sponsored by UNESCO to discuss the peopling of ancient Egypt. He was there with only one other African scholar, Theophile Obenga of the Peoples Republic of the Congo, Brazzaville. Two African and more than 70 European and Arab scholars sat for two days, and when the discussion ended, Diop and Obenga had convincingly demonstrated that Kemet was a "Negro" civilization. There could be no response to their overwhelming arguments. This was the beginning of the end of the historically racist attempt to take Egypt out of Africa and Africans, blacks, out of Egypt. The race paradigm that had tricked Europeans into trying to make Egypt a white or Arab civilization in antiquity collapsed.

REFERENCES AND NOTES

Ambedkar, B. R. (2016). *The annihilation of caste* (Critical ed.). Verso. (Original work published 1936)

> Written by an audacious and insightful observer of the caste system, this provocative book is a critical account of the inherent discrimination in the Hindu caste system.

Ani, M. (1989). *Let the circle be unbroken: The implications of African spirituality in the diaspora*. Red Sea Press.

> This small book was the first indication that Marimba Ani would articulate an innovative approach to the ever-evolving responses of Africans in the Americas to the principles of African spirituality. The introduction of the word *maafa* was just the beginning of the work that she would do to express an Afrocentric perspective on the issues of African historiography. Many of her ideas would emerge in 1994` in the book *Yurugu: An African-Centered Critique of European Cultural Thought and Behavior.*

Ani, M. (1994). *Yurugu: An African-centered critique of European cultural thought and behavior*. Africa World Press.

Azumah, J. A. (2001). *The legacy of Arab-Islam in Africa: A quest for inter-religious dialogue*. One World.

Azumah approaches this sensitive topic in the Islamic world with a quest for dialogue. Of course, one can see that such a dialogue, as it is with other religions, could be difficult because each religion establishes outsiders, those who are victimized by the religion because they do not express allegiance. What Azumah makes clear is that Islam, especially in the relationship of Arabs to Africans, has been problematic.

Ben-Levi, A. J. (1986). The first and second intermediate periods in Kemetic history. In M. Karenga and J. Carruthers (Eds.), *Kemet and the African worldview: Research, rescue and restoration* (pp. 55–69). University of Sankore Press.

Blumenbach, J. F. (1969). *On the natural varieties of mankind* (T. Bendyshe, Trans.). Bergman. (Original work published 1795)

Bynum, E. B. (2012). *The African unconscious: Roots of ancient mysticism and modern psychology*. Cosimo Books.

Bynum remains one of the few African American psychologists outside of the Afrocentrists, such as Joseph White, Na'im Akbar, Linda James Myers, Wade Nobles, and Kofi Kambon, who probed the nature of the roots of the African *sakhu*.

Chandler, W. B. (1988). The jewel in the lotus: The Ethiopian presence in the Indus Valley Civilization. In R. Rashidi & I. Van Sertima (Eds.), *African presence in early Asia* (pp. 80–105). Transaction Books.

Chinweizu. (2010). Lugardism, UN imperialism and the prospect of African power. In A.-O. Dukuzumurenyi (Ed.), *Chinweizu articles*. Lagos.

Darwin, C. (1981). *The descent of man, and selection in relation to sex*. Princeton University Press. https://doi.org/10.5962/bhl.title.2092 (Original work published 1871)

Darwin, C. (1982). *On the origin of species by means of natural selection, or the preservation of favoured races in the struggle for life*. Penguin Books. https://doi.org/10.5962/bhl.title.68064 (Original work published 1859)

Darwin, C. (2014). *The voyage of the beagle*. Skyhorse. (Original work published 1839)

Prior to becoming famous for his studies on evolution and survival, Darwin traveled the world on the Beagle for five years in search of answers about geology, biology, and animals. Indeed, beginning in 1831, Darwin, from a middle-class background, found the time to make an independent research voyage on board the Beagle. The results of his notes are published in this book.

Davis, D. B. (1966). *Slavery and human progress*. Oxford University Press.

Diop, C. A. (1974). *The African origin of civilization*. Lawrence Hill.

Diop, C. A. (1992). *Civilization or barbarism: An authentic anthropology* (Y.-L. M. Ngemi, Trans.). Chicago Review Press.

Dove, N. (1995). An African centered critique of Marx's logic. *Western Journal of Black Studies, 19*(3), 260–271.

Dove, N. (2015). Cultural imperialism. In M. J. Shujaa & K. J. Shujaa (Eds.), *The SAGE encyclopedia of African cultural heritage in North America*. Sage.

Fairservis, W. A., Jr. (1988). The script of the Indus Valley Civilization. In R. Rashidi & I. Van Sertima (Eds.), *African presence in early Asia* (pp. 64–79). Transaction Books.

Fanon, F. (2008). *Black skin, white masks* (R. Philcox, Trans.). Grove Atlantic. (Original work published 1952)

> In this book, that the racist perceptions of black people also cause a moral injury to black people by creating self-hatred and a lack of respect for African culture. As a psychologist, he could see that people affected by their skin color and who wore the mask could be mentally incapacitated.

Gould, S. J. (1981). *The mismeasure of man*. Pelican.

Hart, R. (2002). *Slaves who abolished slavery*. University of the West Indies Press.

> We have found Hart's book penetrating and revealing in its citations and discussions of the resistance movement orchestrated by Africans in the Americas. Nanny of Jamaica, Dessalines of Haiti, Zumbi of Brazil, Yanga of Mexico, and Nat Turner of Virginia, all share in the desire to be free from the shackles of enslavement.

Hunwick, J. O. (1985). *Shari'a in Songhay: The replies of al-Maghili to the questions of Askia Al-Hajj Muhhamed*. New York University Press.

> Hunwick was one of the first to see how ironic it was that sexuality for the African woman was the way to life while the de-sexing of the African man through castration was meant to be a way to live.

Jackson, J. G. (2015). *Introduction to African civilizations*. Ravenio Books. (Original work published 1937)

Jok, M. (2001). *War and slavery in Sudan*. University of Pennsylvania. https://doi.org/10.9783/9780812200584

Knox, R. (2014). *The races of man: A fragment*. Nabu Press. https://doi.org/10.1037/12036-000 (Original work published 1850)

Lewis, B. (1971). *Race and color in Islam*. Joanna Cotler Books.

Lewis, B. (1990). *Race and slavery in the Middle East: An Historical Enquiry*. Oxford University Press.

> Here, Lewis seeks to answer the question of Islam's holding on to enslavement of Africans as European regions of the world abandoned the practice. He particularly sees evidence of this continuation in regions such as Sudan, Mauritania, and possibly Libya and Chad. His notion of the Middle East includes North Africa.

Lewis, B. (1997). *The Middle East: A brief history of the last 2,000 years*. Scribner's.

> Lewis lays down the principal talking points for a discussion of Islam's relationship to questions of race, color, and non-Arab Muslims. This book serves

as the landmark for historiography in the Arab world. Although the idea of "The Middle East" can be questioned as a political rather than a geographical area with any real meaning, the book remains a useful point of entry into the various strands of Islamic thinking.

Lindqvist, S. (2007). *Exterminate all the brutes* (J. Tate, Trans.). New Press. (Original work published 1992)

Written in a passionate manner, this book by Sven Lindqvist, one of Sweden's major thinkers, places the negative perception of Africans right at the door of Europe. It is clear that Lindqvist had the intention of demonstrating that deeply embedded in European thinking are ideas antithetical to cooperative living with Africans.

Long, E. (2011). *The history of Jamaica.* Cambridge University Press. (Original work published 1774)

Ngubane, J. K. (1979). *Conflict of minds: Changing power dispositions in South Africa.* Books in Focus.

Poe, R. (1997). *Black spark, white fire.* Prima.

Heralded in its publication as one of the few times a white American scholar would have the courage to tell the truth about the origin of civilization, Poe's work established the importance of viewing human history and civilization from another perspective. Rich in stories and details of historical interest, *Black Spark, White Fire* tells the story of the origins of Africa and its influences on the world.

Rajshekar, B. T. (1987). *Dalits, black untouchables of India.* Clarity Press.

Rashidi, R., & Van Sertima, I. (Eds.). (1988). *The African presence in early Asia.* Transaction.

A remarkable work by African scholars who organized writers from around the world to make a commentary on the presence of Africans in China, India, Japan, and other Asian lands. Of course, it is clear that the origin of the *Homo sapiens* of Asia is the continent of Africa, just as it is for the rest of the world.

Rushton, J. P. (1997). *Race, evolution, and behavior: A life history perspective.* Transaction.

Said, E. (2003). *Orientalism.* Penguin.

In Said's estimation, the Orient, the region he sees adjacent to Europe, occupies a space in the minds of Europeans principally because of colonies, sources for languages and cultures, and cultural competition. However, for us, it is clear that Said's orientalism is problematic because of its capture of Africa's classical civilizations in an attempt to make a donation to Asia or Europe. Egypt is clearly on the African continent, and the ancient Nile Valley civilizations are in any rational evaluation African civilizations that predate Christianity and Islam.

Shujaa, M. J. (Ed.). (1996). *Beyond desegregation: The politics of quality in African American schooling* (New Frontiers in Urban Education). Corwin Press.

Shujaa, M. J. (Ed.). (1998). *Too much schooling, too little education: A paradox of black life in white societies*. Africa World Press.

> Shujaa became one of the major philosophers of education in the 1990s when he promoted the idea that African children were not being educated but were being "schooled," housed in the building and given instruction that amounted to disinformation and other information that was anti-African.

Stone, M. (1976). *When God was a woman*. Harvest/Hbj.

> Clearly, evidence from archaeology and the earliest written scripts, particularly the sacred texts of the ancient Africans from Kemet and Nubia, shows the emergence and reign of women as deities. The religion of women deities was far more powerful than is generally known. Furthermore, the ancient concepts from the Nile Valley showed that the roles of women in the ancient systems of Africa were more prominent than in either Christianity or Islam.

Thornton, R. (1987). *American Indian holocaust and survival*. University of Oklahoma Press.

> This book explains the extent of the injury done to the North American Indian population during the massive invasion of the Europeans, who saw themselves working out a vision of a new country stretching across the lands of the First Nations from sea to sea. It is impossible to forget that the local populations of the First Nations declined quickly after the hostile encounters with the Europeans, who sought to destroy the people in order to inhabit their lands.

Tolmacheva, M. (1986). Toward the definition of the term Zanj. *Azania: Archaeological Research in Africa*, *21*(4), 105–113. https://doi.org/10.1080/00672708609511371

Volney, C. F. (1950). *Volney's ruins of empires and the law of nature: The ruins, or meditation on the revolutions of empires*. Truth Seeker. (Original work published 1791)

> Volney traveled to Egypt and saw the achievements of African civilizations and went back to Europe believing that all of the arts and sciences, including writing and medicine, had been developed by the black people "we now hold in servitude."

Welsing, F. C. (1991). *The Isis papers*. Third World Press.

> Welsing's analysis of anti-black racism proved to be one of the most provocative examinations of the imagination and behaviors of white Americans. Her works, based on her own experiences as a psychiatrist, helped pierce the veal that had been covering the discourse around race and sex. Falsely criticized by believers in white supremacy, Welsing remained a humanist with an eye toward revealing to white Americans their anti-black behavior in her Cress theory of color-confrontation and racism. Often the pushback was severe and controversial, but she believed that her theories, much as those of Freud in another time, would come to be seen as true.

CHAPTER 3

The Illusive Nature of Race

In 2019, the Detroit educator Dr. Mostafa Hefny, a nationalized American, born in Egypt of African Nubian ancestry, published a book, *I Am Not a White Man but the US Government Is Forcing Me to Be One*, detailing his struggle with the government's racial classification system. Hefny writes,

> In 1987, Wayne County RESA issued to its employees a "Race/Ethnic Identification Card" on which I stated that I am Black. The Director of Human of Human Resources sent me a letter informing me that I am White, not Black and cited Directive 15 of the Office of Management and Budget. (p. 5)

Hefny said that the letter also threatened his career if he did not change the classification from black to white. Directive No. 15 of the Office of Management and Budget (1997) claims that "white people are those having origins in Europe, the Middle East, and North Africa." Obviously, in Hefny's celebrated case and others, this regulation makes no sense;

however, since it is trying to rationalize an impossible situation, it ends up looking quite irrational. This is an old problem in the American nation, one that is almost as old as the country, because it deals with counting who is in the country.

Since the first American census was taken on August 2, 1790, as mandated by Article I, Section 2 of the Constitution, the Census has always been a document comprising racial dimensions. The first census was born with two defects: (1) the counting of an African person as three fifths of a white man and (2) the prohibition against counting Indians, the Native people, who were being massacred at an alarming rate.

Each succeeding census seemed to project the political climate of the time. The 1850 census took social statistics on crime, education, and taxes. And it would not be until 1890 that Indians were counted, 100 years after the first census, by which time their numbers had declined drastically. In 1940, the census takers asked people the number of children ever born to a woman, about internal migration, and whether someone was a veteran.

The dynamic nature of the census is best illustrated by what has happened to the Spanish-speaking population. In 1930, Mexicans were counted, and then in 1940, persons whose mother tongue was Spanish were counted, and then by 1950 and 1960, people with a Spanish surname were enumerated. By 1970, the census was allowing persons to choose from among Mexican, Puerto Rican, Cuban, and other Hispanic classification if they were Spanish speakers. In 1990, the census added nearly 30 Hispanic groups.

Given the knotty history of census taking in a race-conscious society, it is no wonder that most people have not commented on the current census form's racial classifications. The most obvious and questionable issue is the one regarding race. This is what the 2020 census form asked Americans:

The Illusive Nature of Race

> **United States Census Form 2020**
>
> *Select one or more boxes AND enter origins. For this census, Hispanic origins are not races.*
> Top of Form
>
> White
> *Enter, for example, German, Irish, English, Italian, Lebanese, Egyptian, etc.*
>
> Black or African American
> *Enter, for example, African American, Jamaican, Haitian, Nigerian, Ethiopian, Somali, etc.*
>
> American Indian or Alaska Native
> *Enter name of enrolled or principal tribe(s), for example, Navajo Nation, Blackfeet Tribe, Mayan, Aztec, Native Village of Barrow Inupiat Traditional Government, Nome Eskimo Community, etc.*
>
> Asian
> *Enter Chinese, Filipino, Asian Indian, Vietnamese, Korean, Japanese and other Asian.*
> Bottom of Form

The presence of "Egyptian" in the census under the title "White" appears disingenuous until one knows how the Office of Budget Management has defined race in the United States. Claiming someone from an African nation as *white* would not have happened in 1790 or 1990. This was a deliberate political action that confused people about Africa's classical civilizations. Ancient Egypt was not a "white" or "European" civilization, although to claim that Egyptians are white seems to imply that Egypt must be considered a white nation. One could say that the contemporary term "Egyptian" is like saying "American," a term indicating citizenship, not race. Under the American race paradigm, one can be of any race and still be an American. The most ancient "Egyptian race" has always been *black*, not white. In 2020, most of the people who live in Egypt are of Arab background, but the census form does not say "Arab"; it says "Egyptian," which is not only a mistake but a denial of Africa's own classical civilization. "Egyptian" in contemporary parlance indicates the citizenship of the country of Egypt, just like an American can be of Japanese, Italian, or Nigerian origin.

However, the ancient Egyptians were not white. Today's Arabs in Egypt are not Africans; they are also not the people who built the pyramids but rather those who came after General El As marched into Egypt in 639 CE to assist the Africans in throwing off Roman control. They came from Arabia with the religion of Islam and the language of Arabia. They neither spoke the Egyptian language nor identified with the black people of Egypt as Africans; even today, Arabs in Egypt identify not with Africa, although living in Africa, but with Arabia. The U.S. Census may have been more correct to include "Arab" under "White" and to have taken the nationalities Lebanese and Egyptian off of the census form.

If the Arab population is considered *white*, that is one thing, but to claim the citizenship Egyptian as white is deliberately misleading and confusing. The black people who still live in Egypt after thousands of years would not claim whiteness. They are citizens of Egypt but not Arabs. Hence, they are Egyptians by citizenship and African by heritage. From its inception, the American society has sought to enlarge the definition of whiteness, but in the 2020 U.S. Census, with the appropriation of the term "Egyptian" as of the white race, the hubris is clear. Only with this overview is the plight of Mostafa Hefny understandable in the racial paradigm. A society based on race must constantly be on guard against increases and decreases in certain races. How to enlarge the white racial population has been the evolutionary trajectory of the census makers for a century. Once, Italians, Irish, and Jews were not considered white. Yet the elasticity of the racial ladder has meant that only two rungs are permanently fixed, whites at the top and blacks at the bottom. All other rungs can be tampered with at the will of the authorities. Actually, our objective has to be the obliteration of the racial ladder and the enhancing of a common humanity. Of course, it's humanity with difference but not with ranking differences.

Science is the most reasonable platform for understanding our reality. To this end, it is essential that we have a grasp of the facts of human origin and emergence on the African continent before we examine the profile of the illusion called race. It is to science that we must go to discover the truth about the commonality of humanity despite the centuries-long quest to disprove our common humanity. Dove (2018) argues that European academics had taken seriously their campaign "to prove scientifically that humans are distinctly different, based largely on skin color" (p. 130).

The Latin term *Homo sapiens* is translated into English as "wise human being." The word *Homo* means "human being," and the word *sapiens* means "judicious" or "sensible." Given to the modern European languages in 1758 by Carl Linnaeus, one of the notable culprits in the construction of ranking, the term *Homo sapiens* represents the only extant human species. No one has found any living examples of the extinct species of the genus *Homo*, such as *Homo erectus* or *Homo antecessor*. Only *Homo sapiens sapiens*, anatomically modern humans, can claim to represent the ancestral populations of all present humans.

What we know is that the earliest fossil discoveries showing evidence of *Homo sapiens* appear in Africa about 300,000 years ago (Brown et al., 2012). The expansion of *Homo sapiens* from Africa occurred between 30,000 and 100,000 years ago. One of the oldest known skeletons of early modern humans is the Omo Kibish I, which dates to 196,000 years before our era. Of course, there are pieces of other fossils, such as the one found in the Jebel Irhoud region of Morocco from 300,000 years ago and the Florisbad Skull from South Africa, that appear older (McDougall et al., 2008). The Omo remains from Ethiopia date variously between

250,000 and 200,000 years ago (Aubert et al., 2012; Shea, 2008). As of 2020, the scientific consensus seems to be that *Homo sapiens sapiens* rose between 350,000 and 260,000 years ago with the convergence of humans from South Africa and East Africa (McDougall et al., 2005; Pearson et al., 2008).

No human living today is devoid of this continental African origin according to all DNA studies. Humans originated in Africa, spent more than half of the time of *Homo sapiens sapiens* on the continent of Africa, and left Africa as humans to people the earth. The Human Genome Project found in 2003 that there are 3 billion base pairs of genetic letters. Although there are slight nuances or variations, scientists have continued to support the argument that we are the same.

We have consulted, in the previous chapter, with numerous authorities in the ancient world to establish the origins of the race paradigm as it emerged in the attribution of traits, values, and attitudes to human beings on the basis of separate physical characteristics. It may not have been called "race" in ancient times, but the groundwork was being laid for its creation as a construct. The seed sown since those times has matured, been stunted, and then regenerated from time to time, so that in the current period we are battling to establish the earliest ideas of a common humanity. Africans neither invented nor spread the race paradigm. Now that it is regularly called an illusion, a social construct with limited substance in science, we are proposing a return to the Diopian notion of a common humanity as a way of dismantling the false construction of race. Now that we know race is not biological in the sense that there are no genes exclusive to all people called black or white, it is clear that in a genetic sense, racial classifications are not constant, because race is a social construct. Social scientists have distinguished the social construct by markers like complexion, hair texture, eye characteristics, or group identity and by attached construction of traits such as intelligence, talent, ability to work, or genetic superiority or inferiority. Of course, when this is policy, it has consequences and tangible effects (Kendi, 2016) because prejudices can be set in legislation, rules, and regulations. Racist policies do not discriminate against colors; they discriminate against blacks and those who are allies to blacks.

In an article in *The New York Times*, Angela Onwuachi-Willig (2016) made the following statement about how those called white are often made to accept a new reality when in black–white marriages:

> In a society where being white (regardless of one's socioeconomic class background or other disadvantages) means living a life with white skin privileges—such as being presumed safe, competent and noncriminal—whites who begin to experience discrimination because of their intimate connection with someone of another race, or who regularly see their loved ones fall prey to racial discrimination, may begin to no longer feel white. After all, their lived reality does not align with the social meaning of their whiteness.

Therefore, whites who are intimate with blacks are seen in the race paradigm as race traitors because they have chosen to associate with those who are considered less than whites. Historically, whites in the South labeled such whites as "nigger lovers," an epithet that could bring criticism, ostracization, and even punishment to the white person so named. It was necessary for the white population to maintain the illusion that white was superior, and whenever a white person had intimacy with a black person, the racists felt an existential threat.

Lillian Smith (1949/1994) explored the emergence of racial consciousness in the whites of the South by examining her own childhood as a person who grew up with two mothers, one white and one black, both showing affection to her as a child. However, the painful disengagement with the black mother marked a particular line in the development of racial consciousness. The killers of the dream of freedom and liberation must be found in white men who championed the idea of white racial purity while sleeping with black women and abusing black men (Smith, 1994). Of course, the themes of Smith's book are numerous, but they keep converging on the issue of white racial domination of black people. Her point is that after the end of the Civil War the southerners never relinquished the dream of hierarchy, segregation, and white racial purity. All the policies they could create, as Kendi has explained, were meant to demonstrate that the separation of whites and blacks with whites being superior had been, as Jefferson Davis said, "stamped from the beginning." Segregation, an American apartheid system, was meant to nurture white supremacy and racial separation. Smith understood that children were being programmed or brainwashed to continue the racial code, so much so that it appeared that adherence to it was a natural part of their existence. Of course, as she saw and wrote, it was false and damaging to the whites and blacks in the American South. Aiming to keep the hierarchy that had only been bruised during the Civil War, whites in the South ensured through laws and codes that blacks would remember their place as being subservient to whites. They sought to enshrine by practice the rules that would govern both blacks and whites in social relations. Certain attitudes were taboo and had to be punished, even until death if necessary. Every institution in the South had to conform to this ideology of superiority. Schools and churches enforced these social constructs, and the churches, both black and white, had images of the white Jesus throughout their buildings to support the malady of massive racial demagoguery. The ethics was tainted, the religion racist, and the ideas unscientific.

Personal associations underscore the problem with the idea of race tagged to traits. Whether it is in the material market of home ownership or business loans, black people are deemed, as part of the race syndrome, riskier than whites by many banks. Black people are considered contagious, and if a bank makes loans to black people, it might find itself marked by whites as being a poorly run or marginal bank, without any real evidence. Of course, what does happen at times is that the property of black people is often redlined, that is, considered an area that is dangerous for a bank to make loans. Consequently, a black family that buys a house in what was originally a white neighborhood that became predominantly black might lose the original value of the house as the area is redlined; that is, property is lowered in value simply because banks decide that they do not want to make loans to buyers in a black neighborhood. Hence, the property has not changed, but the perception of the owners, blacks, is negative. Perhaps one of the most poignant responses to the question of discrimination was given by the philosopher James Baldwin when a British reporter asked him if he felt that he had been discriminated because he was black and he answered, "No, not because I am black but because I am despised."

The reader will remember that we have discussed the iconography of race from ancient times, but we see it explicitly in this age with the Christian idea of a white Jesus with blue eyes and a black devil with a pitchfork in his hands: What could be more deeply disturbing to Africans than these images showing the devil as black and god as white? Only where blacks have been colonized and subjugated can such images continue to dominate the landscape.

How do we prevent the creation and generation of mental enslavement and coloniality? This has to be one of the agenda items of African world philosophers. Too many Africans are agents of Europeanization, whereby they have taken on the race paradigm. One could argue that humans are free to choose a culture, but if one chooses based on abandoning one's own culture, it is human capitulation to the race paradigm. All humanity should answer the cultural questions that sit at the head of existence:

Who are you?
Where are you?
To whom are you speaking?
Who said you were naked?
Where are your clothes?

The above questions are fundamental concerns when it comes to the issue of culture. "Who are you?" deals with ancestry and lineage. "Where are you?" deals with location and geography? To whom are you speaking about values, interests, and visions? Who gave you opinions on the state of your material condition? With whom do you trade and find clothes, goods, and products? The answers to the cultural questions do not involve issues of color, creed, gender, or class. They are straightforward and direct.

The Uses and Misuses of Race

While we have seen that the foundations for racial distinctions were laid in the ancient texts and traditions of non-African people, race itself was not promoted as such until the 16th century, when Europeans sought to rationalize their military and commercial conquests by appealing to the consequences of superiority and inferiority of races.

Race is not the same as caste or the ethnocentrisms that preceded it in various regions of the world. For example, it was possible for a Han Chinese to see others in Asia as barbarians who had to be shut out by the Great Wall because they did not speak the language; in India, the Hindus created an enormously complex system of separating people by the caste in which they were born and from which they could not escape in life. As we have discussed in Chapter 1, dispossession, abuse, exploitation, and attempts to dehumanize groups by suggesting disfavor for them by the conquerors existed before race, but we agree that "no other historical or ethnographic order, however, has been as globally inclusive in its assignment of social and cultural difference to natural causes as has post-1400s racism" (Sanjek, 1994, p. 4). It appears that culture and race were not so tightly interlinked as they would become under the exploitative reign of the enslavers and colonizers. Race to modern Europeans became a globalized system of exploitation based on the ranking of groups of people from various regions of the world. Race in the American nation was complicated by the pandemic of enslavement, but the infamous landmarks of injustice became marks of negativity in the march toward dispensing with false racial perceptions based on the racial ladder. Take, for example, the setup for a reign of terror against African people during the 19th century, when the legal apparatus of the American government sought to maintain the indefensible position that Africans should be seen as less than white people.

Infamy in the Racial Ladder

In 1834, a 35-year old enslaved African, Dred Scott, was taken from Missouri, a slave state, to Illinois, a free state, and then to Wisconsin, a territory that did not have slavery as a result of the Missouri Compromise of 1820, whereby the proslavery politicians worked out an agreement with the antislavery politicians to split the new territories between the two conditions. Scott lived in Wisconsin with his slave owner, Dr. John Emerson, and his wife for several years and then returned to Missouri. Emerson died in 1846, and Scott sued Emerson's widow for his freedom, saying that he had lived as a free person in a free territory for several years. The lower court granted him his rights, but the Missouri Supreme Court reversed the ruling, claiming that he was still enslaved.

Not one to give up on his claim to freedom, Scott appealed the decision to a federal court since his new owner, J. F. A. Sanford, was a resident of New York. The federal court accepted the case on the basis of the diversity of states represented in the case. However, the lower federal court decided against Scott. The case then went to the U.S. Supreme Court, where a bitter division existed between the antislavery and majority proslavery justices.

In the end, the court ruled on March 6, 1857, that the Constitution did not include citizenship for black people, whether enslaved or free, and that there were no rights and privileges conferred on white Americans that had to be conferred on black people. Basically, what the Court decided was that Scott as a black person had no legal right to ask for his freedom.

It would not be until near the end of the American Civil War in 1865 that Africans would gain legal citizenship, but even then, there was a shakiness in the granting of freedom and citizenship. The Thirteenth

Amendment to the U.S. Constitution abolished slavery and involuntary servitude, *except as punishment for a crime*. Although the amendment was passed by Congress on January 31, 1865, and ratified by the required 27 of the then 36 states on December 6, 1865, and proclaimed on December 18, white legislators, sheriffs, and courts did not waste any time in criminalizing black people to re-enslave blacks by another way.

On July 9, 1868, the Fourteenth Amendment to the Constitution was ratified. It formally granted citizenship to all persons "born or naturalized in the United States," including former enslaved persons, and provided all citizens with "equal protection under the laws." It authorized the government to punish states that abridged citizens' right to vote by proportionally reducing their representation in Congress, and it prohibited people who "engaged in insurrection" against the United States from holding any civil, military, or elected office without the approval of two thirds of the House and Senate. Ultimately, little of this mattered when it came to the treatment of African people in the country.

Almost 25 years later in 1892, Homer Plessy, a man considered in the race paradigm a person of seven-eighths white and one-eighth African ancestry, who was a resident of New Orleans, deliberately violated the transportation code by riding on a "whites only" railcar. He was charged for violating the New Orleans Separate Car Act of 1890. His lawyers defended him on the grounds that the law was unconstitutional. He lost in the first court trial and then lost again at the Louisiana Supreme Court. At the U. S. Supreme Court, the decision of May 1896 was one of the worst decisions ever by a Supreme Court. It affirmed all the lower courts, saying that punishing Plessy did not violate the Fourteenth Amendment, which established legal equality of black and white Americans. The Court voted 7-1 against Plessy, claiming that the Fourteenth Amendment could not eliminate "all social distinctions" and that state legislatures had the right to determine laws that regulated health, safety, and morals.

The lone dissenter, Justice John Marshall Harlan, wrote that the U. S. Constitution "is color-blind, and neither knows nor tolerates classes among citizens." Harlan's position was that the New Orleans Separate Car Act should have been found unconstitutional.

Protecting the racial ladder weighed heavily on the justices as they affirmed their support for the illusion of the purity of the white race, the one drop of African blood disqualification from equal treatment, and the ability of states to still use social distinctions. It would take the 1954 *Brown v. Topeka Board of Education* to start to undo the "separate but equal" doctrine as unconstitutional in public schools and facilities. The legal system can never work unless the people who work it abandon the idea of two types and levels of justice, one for whites and one for blacks.

If science says that all *Homo sapiens* are 99.9% the same, we must ask ourselves, how did we come to the point of race or races and the establishment of the system of racism? The worst examples of violent bloodshed and savagery have occurred around the ranking of our miniscule differences. As we shall see, the political agenda of demagogues and dictators has always included the overturning of our common humanity for a fudging of differences to defeat the sameness found in humanity. This is why, especially in Europe and America, the misuse of biology has produced practitioners of eugenics and other disciplines, imaginary or false, to support ideas of domination and white supremacy.

In 1883, just barely a year before the Berlin Conference of 1884–1885, the British scholar Sir Francis Galton coined the term "eugenics" and started a movement that sought to selectively breed humans to make "better" people. Galton, a cousin of Charles Darwin, believed that it is necessary to choose the desired characteristics of humans and breed them. Studying the British upper class, Galton concluded that the highest positions in society were based on good genetic composition. His ideas, while not considered significant in the United Kingdom, took on a strong following in the racialized United States.

In the United States, the eugenics movement concentrated on weeding out so-called undesirable elements so that they would not be transmitted to the next generation. While this attitude resonated with the white supremacist policies in the United States and gained sponsorship from private and corporate funders, it also caused others to object to the recording of family histories for the purposes of eugenicist actions. Policies were enacted against immigration that would bring "undesirables" into the country, African people were seen as a drag on the society because of pauperism and other traits that were attributed to genetics, and there was advocacy for sterilizing the so-called unfit. Tracking family histories to prove the validity of the thesis and to "correct" the genetic line might be said to have encouraged the Nazi experiments on those who were alcoholics, mentally ill, deaf, blind, or known for sexual promiscuity. Certainly, the slaughter of the Jews must be seen in the same light of racism as the genetic doctrine of white supremacy. Many African American women were sterilized during medical procedures without being given anesthesia. Although the eugenics movement lost favor in the United States when it was seen that Hitler used the same principles to justify his attacks on Jews, Romas, homosexuals, Afro-Germans, the blind, the deaf, and handicapped people, it had nevertheless proved that it found a fertile ground in American society.

As we have seen, the strand of racial hierarchy inherited by contemporary society reaches back beyond the Greek experience; yet it is the ancient Greeks, with their knowledge of certain African values, as per the *Histories* by Herodotus, who gave the modern Europeans some impetus for their emphasis on ideas of naturalism in regard to the relationships between humans. Aristotle proclaimed in *Politics* that certain other philosophers disdained the idea that some people by using brute force had the right to master those with less strength, although in his own mind there was a case to be made for "virtuous" slaveholding because it was a natural idea. Herein is one of the gems of this arduous road to an errant country of unnatural relationships where one people have been granted or have taken the right to rule over others.

It should be clear by now that nowhere in Ancient Kemet was there a construction of relationships like the one created by patriarchy. This was obviously not an African concept because nowhere in any of the texts of Egypt do we discover information that would allow us to render some people naturally masters and others naturally slaves. However, centuries after Aristotle and during the enslavement of Africans for 246 years in the United States, for 300 years in Brazil, and in other countries, Europeans, harking back to what was called classical Greece, reestablished a neoclassical attitude about knowledge. Noticeably, to Afrocentrists, this harking back did not go to the beginning of science, scholarship, and mathematics but to certain Greeks, namely Socrates, Plato, and Aristotle. The latter was, of course, farther away from the realities of life in Ancient Kemet and did not seem to have had the same understanding as Socrates and Plato about the ancient civilization. It was Aristotle after all who said in *Physiognomonica* that the Egyptians and Ethiopians were cowards because too black a hue makes one a coward. Taking their lead and impetus from Aristotle, the Americans, North and South, found solace in their stand that it was natural for whites to rule over blacks.

Anthropology has a special place in the pantheon of disciplines that support the idea of human separation in terms of races. Stephen Jay Gould's classic work *The Mismeasure of Man* (1981) was written in demonstration of the history of racial ranking as a part of the intellectual process in the West. Lee D. Baker was one of the first to write about the central role played by anthropology in shaping America's racist history. His book *From Savage to Negro: Anthropology and the Construction of Race, 1896–1954* (1998), based on his Temple University dissertation, remains one of the key works detailing how an academic discipline contributed to notions of biological difference and ranking. Clearly, Baker believed that Franz Boas, the legendary anthropologist, made a major contribution to the field of anthropology by delinking race, language, and culture. While this was useful, Boas was seen as somewhat of a progressive by many blacks because he argued that people did not move from savage to barbarism to culture; rather, Boas saw that cultural differences accounted for much more than race or the "evolution" from one state to another. Africans came to America with thousands of years of history and culture, and the idea of biological determination where nothing would change meant that even barbarism among the whites was bound to be a fact of life forever. However, many anthropologists took the position that certain environmental factors could have an impact on people's human potential as well as their cultural development in some ways. Thus, some whites believed that black people could be Christianized and educated and therefore become civilized; others, however, believed that Africans, Italians, Jews, and Irish were all impossible to change and hence they would be held in place to the end of time.

One culture is neither greater nor better than another. All cultures have been formed and are forming along lines that are necessary in the relevant environments and elements of the people. The complexity of one is similar to the complexity of another, and hence all are equally significant in their own merits. Our plan is to put forth an idea about culture that suggests the intricacies of the Amharas, Danish, Lenape, Muskogee, Celts, and African Brazilians will reveal the same complexity, regularity, and usefulness. Only in this way can we begin to look at cultures as relative to one another, that is, different but without ranking in a hierarchical fashion.

The Functioning of the Race Paradigm

There are many descriptions of the reigning racial paradigm one finds, for example, in the United States. Clearly, the idea that one human group asserts the power to dis-authorize and de-enthrone another group from humanity while hyper-authorizing its own group is the common description of how race works as a system. It should be pointed out that although there was ushered into the scholarly and speculative arena of race during the 1970s and 1980s a strong reaction with the terms "ethnicity" and "minority," as conservative intellectuals sought ways to minimize the oppressive nature of racism, even those terms carried so much weight that they could not lighten the burden that had already been laden on race. Some saw this shift to ethnicity, for example, as a "neo-conservative glorification of ethnicity" to downplay the emphasis on racism (see Kristol, 1966). Of course, this was not the truth, and the falsity of this proposition could be pointed out in many ways. Africans did not make a choice to come to the Americas. Kristol (1966) was definitely only comparing blacks with European immigrants, not with Asian and other African groups that also came to America. Most freshmen in college can demonstrate the inaccuracy of this comparison. However, a move to say that the disputes between Hausa and Fulani, or the Tigreans, Oromo, and Amharas, were just like the "race" issues between whites and blacks in America could never meet the taste test; race was something so totally ingrained in the soil of the American philosophy of society that it would take a different reconceptualization to deal with it adequately, and ethnicity was not that coin. At any rate, the truth is that many white "ethnics" quickly lost their attachments to their ethnic roots in the quicksand of America's racial quagmire. Some European ethnic groups, after a couple of generations in the United States, complain that they cannot even pronounce their last names correctly (Sanjek, 1994). In effect, the ethnic identities of Europeans collapsed into a pool of whiteness after a couple of generations and started the process of racial oppression against Africans anew, if it had ever stopped in the first place.

The idea of race served several mistresses and masters; principal among them was eugenics. A history of the eugenics movement proves that what was inherited in the ancient mythology of old civilizations in Asia and Europe became the template for the construction of new forms of the same oppression based on the hierarchy of "races." To put it plainly, the abuse, subjugation, and attempted dehumanization of Africans remain at the core of all social systems involving Europeans and Africans, even if in some respects the victims of persecution and oppression might also be other people from time to time. We believe that the defeat of prejudice, the overcoming of all euphemisms that support the race paradigm, like "duality," "plural societies," "people of color," and so forth, will require a new, nonhierarchical understanding of humanity where *Homo sapiens* is the category for all people and distinctions of culture are created for discussions about human organization and innovation.

Nevertheless, we recognize that we are fighting through the numerous palisades that have been set up to protect this racial regime. It is as if the racial ladder has been implanted into the human brain. Take the situation almost anywhere in the Americas, Africa, and Asia where we have seen European settlements or domination. Those areas have been subjugated to the bad ideas of race. For example, Brazil went to work almost immediately in the 16th century to establish a reign of racial terror where the elites of the society based an entire system on *brancos, pardos, pretos, amarelos*, and indigenous categories. Of course, the *brancos* was considered the favorite of the ranking ladder, next came the *pardos*, and in the bottom rungs were the other categories. Where did the Portuguese get these categories from, and what was the idea behind this type of system? In fact, in some places, all of the categories except whites, *brancos*, were further subdivided into groups depending on their proximity to whites.

It should be clear that this race idea, once unleashed on the world, has led to the acceptance of its murdering dagger by various other nations. It is not something that affects only Europeans, although this is our current and most popular reality; the Arabs have continued the dangerous race paradigm until now it sits in the heart of a country like Sudan and has affected Egypt, Libya, Mauritania, and other nations in the Islamic world. Take the story that Zeinab Mohammed Salih, a brilliant Sudanese journalist, wrote about for the BBC on July 26, 2020. What one sees in this quite typical example is the incredible and horrific racial quagmire that engulfs many countries governed by Arabs. In effect, racism is as abusive among Arabs as it has been among Europeans when it comes to attacks on black people in Sudan. Salih says, "As anti-racism protests swept through various parts of the world following African American George Floyd's death in police custody in the US, Sudan seemed to be in a completely different world" (p. 1). Indeed, she describes accurately the conditions of racism and the influence of the racist paradigm on society when she writes that "the superiority complex of many Arabs lies at the heart of some of the worst conflicts in Sudan." When the popular black soccer player Issam Abdulrajeem married Reem Khougli, a light-complexioned Arab makeup artist, they received vicious attacks and racial slurs. Black Lives Matter (BLM) did not make any difference to the ruling Arab population in Sudan, who ranted against a black man marrying a light-skinned Arab woman. One person wrote on their Facebook page, "Seriously girl, this is *haram*" because a queen does not "marry a slave." The only thing that made this *haram* ("forbidden") was the racist construction that Arabs are superior to Africans. Salih makes it clear that Arab Sudanese newspapers regularly use negative and derogatory slurs in reference to dark-skinned Africans. The observant and thorough Salih anticipates the argument that we are making for humanity when she relates how the Arab head of a women's group called No More Women Oppression nevertheless "commented on a photo showing a young black man with his white European wife by saying that the woman, in choosing her husband, may have been looking for the creature missing on the evolutionary ladder between humans and monkeys." It is ironic that in Africa, where *Homo sapiens* originated and human civilization was first produced, there are now Arabs who glorify the false racial ladder created largely to justify their domination of Africans. Furthermore, there are few organized Arab groups that are aligned with the liberation of the color regime established to protect privilege among the lighter-complexioned Arabs. The lack of documents opposed to crimes against dark-skinned people suggests the continuing acceptance of the false notion of race in the Arab world.

During the African American women–led BLM demonstrations that took place around the world in 2020, the indigenous people of Australia voiced their complaints in the same language as did the African Americans. The BLM and Stop First Nations Deaths in Custody protests across Australia since early June have similarly called for charges against police and prison guards who killed First Nations people in their custody. Racialized murder in Australia seems to follow the same pattern as that found in other European-dominated countries, where the ranking of humans according to physical characteristics has been used to discriminate, abuse, and kill people. The demonstrations in Australia penned their passions to redressing the lack of accountability among the police, who were responsible for 438 deaths of First Nations people between 1991 and 2020. Once again, we are suggesting that there cannot be any structural change until the society has the will to destroy the ideology of white supremacy, which is based on a false myth. The policing organizations reflect the ideology of the superstructure that allows for the demeaning and devaluing of First Nations people. While it is a cliché to say that this is based on the doctrine of white supremacy, the idea of white supremacy comes from the hierarchical ranking and trait notation system of the whites who entered the land of the First Nations with their own racialized mentalities.

Classification of People

Although, as we have shown in Chapters 1 and 2, there was deep and disturbing evidence of human separations and divisions by classification in Europe and Asia, as in the Hebrew, Hindu, Arab, and Greek traditions prior to the 18th century, it was the work of an entire cadre of racially motivated authors who propagated the pejorative notions of a racial ladder with white people at the top and black people at the bottom. Those who promulgated this false notion operated on the basis of centuries of racist propaganda, and those who followed the path that was carved out of the forest of human relationships ended up in the trash bin of irrationality.

Joseph Arthur Comte de Gobineau, a French aristocrat who lived between 1816 and 1882, pushed a racial geography that would constitute legitimacy in Europe and elsewhere for the most heinous crimes committed against humanity. In Gobineau's vision, there was the Aryan master race sitting at the top of the racial ladder. His *Essai sur l'inégalité des races humaines* (*The Inequality of Human Races*, 1855/1915) established him as one of the most articulate rhetoricians of race in his era. He claimed that aristocrats, like himself, were superior to commoners because they possessed more Aryan traits and had fewer incidents of interbreeding with inferior races such as the Alpines and Mediterranean area people. Gobineau's thoughts would become a commonly used meme in the language of white supremacists such as Donald Trump, who was known for saying,

> "Well I think I was born with the drive for success because I have a certain gene. I'm a gene believer. . . . Hey, when you connect two race horses, you usually end up with a fast horse. I had a good gene pool from the standpoint of that, so I was pretty much driven." (Mortimer, 2016)

By virtue of his beliefs, Trump has rightly been called a serial liar, rampant xenophobe, racist, fascist, misogynist, and birther, one who claimed that Barack Obama could not be an American because he was not born in the United States, which was a lie.

While it is not accurate to lay the blame for eugenics and fascist racism only on the Aryan thesis, there is no doubt that Gobineau's popularization of this idea had a major impact on the institutionalization of racist attitudes in the West. It would take a major Haitian polemicist, anthropologist, and Pan Africanist, Anténor Firmin, with his book *De l'égalité des races humaines* (*The Equality of the Human Races*, 1885/2002), to destroy the arguments of Gobineau's racist *Essai sur l'inégalité des races humaines*. Firmin's work circulated among African people and some progressive European intellectuals, yet although it was well argued it did not prevent the spread of Gobineau's ideas, which had decades of rapid promotion among Europeans.

It should be understood that Gobineau's ideas did not leap out of thin air; his ideas had been cultivated by the promotion of the views of a school of European thinkers who had been influenced by the race theories, as we have shown in Chapter 2. Those earlier influences would also have influenced the work of Darwin, whose book *On the Origin of Species by Means of Natural Selection, or the Preservation of Favoured Races in the Struggle for Life* (1859/1982) advanced the theory of evolutionary biology, whereby natural selection was said to choose the fittest for procreation. Today, Darwin's book is often referred to simply as *The Origin of Species* and consequently does not project in that title the notion of "favoured races," which was the conversation in the European's heroic 19th century, when it seemed that with the military conquest of other lands Europe was destined to rule the world.

It would be a mistake for us to assume that this European hubris did not surround the adventures of swashbuckling adventurers, missionaries, gold rushers, and colony-building white men and women who risked their lives to "advance" their race. Such a racist vision saw all other people on the racial ladder as having essential characteristics that placed them on an unchanging rung, whether they were Slavs, Jews, Africans, First Nations, or Aryans.

By the middle of the 20th century, the American anthropologist Carleton Stevens Coon (1962) had entered the arena with his division of humanity into what he called the five races:

1. Caucasoid, or white race
2. Negroid, or black race

3. Capoid, or Bushmen/Hottentot race
4. Mongoloid, or Oriental/Amerindian race
5. Australoid, or Australian Aborigine and Papuan race

In some ways, it was unfortunate that Coon, a leading anthropologist, straddled most of the 20th century while he was leading the racist front of anthropology. A professor at the University of Pennsylvania and Harvard University, Coon was born in 1904 and died in 1981, at which time he was president of the American Association of Physical Anthropology. From this perch, he essentially dominated the thinking in the field of anthropology, and it would be other anthropologists not under his wings who would have to dispute his pseudoscientific theories.

Coon was quite active in advancing his theories, traveling to many countries, serving as a spy for the U.S. government, promoting his theories of race, and eventually publishing *The Races of Europe* in 1939 and *The Origin of Races* in 1962. But it was in his book *The Living Races of Man* (1965) that he asserted that the human species divided into five races before it evolved into *Homo sapiens*. Coon believed that there was a polygenesis of evolution into *Homo sapiens*; that is, different races evolved at different times into *Homo sapiens*. Race typology had just about run its course in the field of anthropology, and both *The Origin of Races* and *The Living Races of Man* were seen as supporting racist ideas with bad theory and few data. The critic Theodore Dobzhansky, a leading anthropologist of the time, thought that Coon was providing argumentative grounds for racists.

Although Dobzhansky had issues with Coon, it should be remembered that Ashley Montagu had a major debate with Dobzhansky over the anthropological use of the term "race." They could not agree on the subject. It was Montagu's belief that "race" had too many toxic associations so it could not be used adequately in science. Dobzhansky argued that science should precisely define the term and not give in to its misuse.

The opinionated Dobzhansky said about Montagu's autobiography, "The chapter on 'Ethnic Group and Race' is, of course, deplorable, but let us say that it is good that in a democratic country any opinion, no matter how deplorable, can be published" (Farber 2015, p. 3). What happened subsequently was that the discussion of race moved toward a focus on gene frequencies in the population rather than morphological "racial types." Although this has been done in science, it seems that social and value prejudices were associated with morphological ideas of race.

Scientists believe that there is more variation between individuals in each genetic population grouping than there is among the groups (Farber, 2011). Farber (2011) suggests that Dobzhansky's believed that "races" had to mix or else they would become different species. All present races were considered products of racial mixing (Farber, 2011). Dobzhansky, a Russian American scientist, had arrived in the United States in the 1920s already a well-published evolutionary biologist; he found that the debate on race in America needed the benefit of scientific discourse, which he attempted to provide (Farber, 2011). His conclusion that human nature could be seen as both biological and cultural and that these two aspects depended on biological and cultural evolution sparked further discussion about the role of biology but did not provoke more running after the race paradigm. In fact, Dobzhansky claimed that biology is something humans shared with other forms of life; however, culture is exclusive to humans.

The False Practice of Race

The U.S. Census Bureau defines race as a person's self-identification with one or more social groups. An individual can report as white, black/African American, Asian, American Indian/Alaskan Native, or Native Hawaiian/Other Pacific Islander. The U.S. Census Bureau defines Hispanic or Latino/a as "a person of Cuban, Mexican, Puerto Rican, South or Central American, or other Spanish culture or origin *regardless of race*." It claims as white "a person having origins in any of the original peoples of Europe, the Middle

East, or North Africa." It includes people who indicate their race as "white" or report origins such as Irish, Egyptian, German, English, Scandinavian, Scottish, Near Easterner, Iranian, Lebanese, or Polish.

Racism is the public policy of the ranking and classification of humanity along lines of physical traits, such as hair texture, eye color, and complexion. And it is the very people who generated this species classification who venerated white supremacy as public policy in religion, education, philosophy, science and technology, trade and commerce, and now in all areas of human life by humiliating "others" to uplift themselves.

REFERENCES AND NOTES

Atlanta Black Star. (2017, December 8). *10 Reasons the enslavement of Africans in Libya should alarm us.* https://atlantablackstar.com/2017/12/08/10-reasons-enslavement-africans-libya/

Aubert, M., Pike, A. W. G., Stringer, C., Bartsiokas, A., Kinsley, L., Eggins, S., Day, M., & Grün, R. (2012). Confirmation of a late middle Pleistocene age for the Omo Kibish I cranium by direct uranium-series dating. *Journal of Human Evolution, 63*(5), 704–710. https://doi.org/10.1016/j.jhevol.2012.07.006

Baker, L. D. (1998). *From savage to Negro: Anthropology and the construction of race, 1896–1954.* University of California Press. https://doi.org/10.1525/9780520920194

Brown v. Board of Education of Topeka, 347 U.S. 483 (1954). https://supreme.justia.com/cases/federal/us/347/483/

Brown, F. H., McDougall, I., & Fleagle, J. G. (2012). Correlation of the KHS Tuff of the Kibish Formation to volcanic ash layers at other sites, and the age of early *Homo sapiens* (Omo I and Omo II). *Journal of Human Evolution, 63*(4), 577–587. https://doi.org/10.1016/j.jhevol.2012.05.014

Coon, C. S. (1939). *The races of Europe.* Macmillan.

Coon, C. S. (1962). *The origin of races.* Random House.

Coon, C. S. (1965). *The living races of man.* Knopf.

Darwin, C. (1982). *On the origin of species by means of natural selection, or the preservation of favoured races in the struggle for life.* Penguin Books. https://doi.org/10.5962/bhl.title.68064 (Original work published 1859)

Dove, N. (2018). Race revisited: Against a cultural construction bearing significant implications. *International Journal of African Renaissance Studies: Multi-, Inter-, and Transdisciplinarity, 13*(2), 129–143. https://doi.org/10.1080/18186874.2018.1538703

In a clear and decisive discourse on race, Dove points out the inadequate nature of previous discourses on race. She establishes that the contradictions inherit in the cultural construction of race make it impossible for race to make meaning in our world.

Farber, P. L. (2011). *Mixing races: From scientific racism to modern evolutionary ideas.* Johns Hopkins University Press.

This is a book about reinventing and re-envisioning the discourse on scientific racism and evolution.

Farber, P. L. (2015). Dobzhansky and Montagu's debate on race: The aftermath. *Journal of the History of Biology, 49*(4), 1–15. https://doi.org/10.1007/s10739-015-9428-1

Firmin, A. (2002). *The equality of the human races* (A. Charles, Trans.). University of Illinois Press. (Original work published 1885)

One of the most important contributions to Pan-African thought, anthropology, and Africology. In his brilliant response to Gobineau, although decades later, Firmin, the great Haitian intellectual, showed himself equal as a thinker and scholar to any person writing in French.

Gobineau, J. A. Comte de. (1915). *The inequality of human races* (A. Collins, Trans.). G. P. Putnam's. (Original work published 1855)

Gould, S. J. (1981). *The mismeasure of man.* Pelican.

Hefny, M. (2019). *I am not a white man but the US government is forcing me to be one.* Africa World Press.

A provocative account of a Nubian/African born in Egypt who has spent more than 30 years fighting the U.S. government's racial classification of him, a black man, as white simply because he was born in Egypt. His phenomenal work to demonstrate the racial animosity against black people in the United States because of the appropriation of ancient African contributions to majestic civilization has pushed this question to the forefront for a lot of activists and intellectuals. Why is it that the U.S. government has sought to describe someone born in North Africa as white when Africa is a black continent?

Kendi, I. X. (2016). *Stamped from the beginning.* Bold Type Books.

A book that confirmed the arrival of Ibram Kendi in the field of African American studies as a serious thinker, historian, and Africologist. He argues that, like Jefferson Davis said, race and racism seem to have been stamped from the beginning. Yet Kendi is an optimist and believes that we must confront the racist history of a country that has for far too long enthroned inequality.

Kristol, I. (1966, September 11). The Negro today is like the immigrant yesterday. *New York Times Magazine*, p. 301. https://contemporarythinkers.org/irving-kristol/essay/the-negro-today-is-like-the-immigrant-yesterday/

McDougall, I., Brown, F. H., & Fleagle, J. G. (2005). Stratigraphic placement and age of modern humans from Kibish, Ethiopia. *Nature, 433*, 733–736. https://doi.org/10.1038/nature03258

McDougall, I., Brown, F. H., & Fleagle, J. G. (2008). Sapropels and the age of hominins Omo I and II, Kibish, Ethiopia. *Journal of Human Evolution, 55*(3), 409–420. https://doi.org/10.1016/j.jhevol.2008.05.012

Mortimer, C. (2016, September 30). Donald Trump believes he has superior genes, biographer claims. *Independent*. https://www.independent.co.uk/news/world/americas/donald-trump-president-superior-genes-pbs-documentary-eugenics-a7338821.html

Office of Budget and Management. (1997, October 30). *Federal Register, 62*(219), Article 58786.

Onwuachi-Willig, A. (2016, September 6). Race and racial identity are social constructs. *The New York Times*. https://www.nytimes.com/roomfordebate/2015/06/16/how-fluid-is-racial-identity/race-and-racial-identity-are-social-constructs

Pearson, O. M., Royer, D. F., Grine, F. E., & Fleagle, J. G. (2008). A description of the Omo I postcranial skeleton, including newly discovered fossils. *Journal of Human Evolution, 55*(3), 421–437. https://doi.org/10.1016/j.jhevol.2008.05.018

Salih, Z. M. (2020, July 26). Viewpoint from Sudan—where blacks are called slaves. *BBC News*. https://www.bbc.com/news/world-africa-53147864

> In a sharp report on the crisis in Sudan, where the Arab minority has sought to express domination over the 90% of black African people, Salih found that the Arab idea of their superiority to Africans constitutes a major problem to overcome for Sudanese peace.

Sanjek, R. (1994). The enduring inequalities of race. In S. Gregory & R. Sanjek (Eds.), *Race* (pp. 46–58). Rutgers University Press.

> Sanjek seeks to analyze the extent of whiteness, privilege, and race mixing, among other themes, to show how inequalities continue to plague American society.

Shea, J. J. (2008). The Middle Stone Age archaeology of the Lower Omo Valley Kibish Formation: Excavations, lithic assemblages, and inferred patterns of early *Homo sapiens* behavior. *Journal of Human Evolution, 3*(55), 444–448. https://doi.org/10.1016/j.jhevol.2008.05.014

Smith, L. (1994). *Killers of the dream*. W. W. Norton. (Original work published 1949)

CHAPTER 4

The Promoters of Racism

Once race had been enthroned in the temple of Western society, it was only a matter of time before it gave birth to racism and the attendant ideologies that would support the structure of white male patriarchy and racial hierarchy. Various institutions, from churches to colleges, and authoritative sources, from politicians to preachers, encouraged by both scientists and quacks, attempted to enshrine forever what had been enthroned as the natural order. Armond Towns (2019) sets this conduct up perfectly while commenting on Marshall McLuhan, the late Canadian philosopher of culture:

> Marshall McLuhan is not your traditional scholar of race. Yet, he seemed preoccupied with the topic. In everything from *The Gutenberg Galaxy* to "The Playboy Interview," McLuhan wrote fervently about race. Whether he was talking about Kenya or Europe; "tribal" or "detribal"; space or time; or "Negro," "Indian," or White men, McLuhan's theories of media have always assumed race, albeit not the most nuanced theory of race. Indeed, McLuhan's

association of Black and Indigenous people as tribal builds off a long history of Western associations of tribalism with a presumed intellectual and racial superiority over Black and Brown people, particularly in anthropology and psychiatry. (pp. 547–548)

What the observant Towns realized was that one of the most important popular cultural theorists of the 20th century could not escape, although he may have tried, the imprisoning tropes of racist societies. Popular culture was essentially draped in the rhetoric of race and the hierarchical structure that had been handed down from generation to generation. McLuhan (1966) knew that the system was stacked decidedly against those people defined as "tribal" because whites had assigned them an inferior position. McLuhan could have predicted precisely why a black 17-year-old could not get Donald Trump Jr. to respond to a black man killing two people and wounding another with the words he used about Kyle Rittenhouse in an appearance on the extratv show on September 8, 2020, when he said, "We all do stupid things at 17." The implication is that a young white man murdering two people is different from a young black man's wayward actions. Is it just stupid that someone murders two people and injures another out of hatred? All of this is a racist construction of the imaginative ladder in the minds of racists who argue that white people must be given a different level of understanding from black people. Our argument is straightforward: Africans did not create this racial ladder and have been seeking ways off of it since the beginning of our encounter with Europeans. Rittenhouse's murders are among the vilest racist types of assault; he came ready for a "race" war and was armed and eager to engage with those he saw as the enemy. Our search for the enemy must always begin with ourselves, but the race paradigm in both its historical and its contemporary sense is about greater than and lesser than, an equation of hatred for human beings.

With white male hierarchy at the top of the racial ladder and white women and girls on the second rung of the "natural" order, the popular cultural manifestations in the Western community utilized the racial ladder to make policy in every sector of society. It all began with the ladder and ended with the ladder in an oxymoronic swirl of insanity passing from one generation to the next, where a large part of the white population believed that they were smarter, better, and more beautiful than all the other people in the world. They would defend this doctrinal delusion as if their lives depended on it. In effect, this belief gave them the idea that they had a "right" to dictate to all other peoples the nature of society, create policies that would protect their privilege, and assert that even God is white. To dispute this construction would make the disputant look like a fool given the overwhelming "evidence" that had been amassed in support of the "favoured" races, as Charles Darwin had said in the title of his famous book *Origin of Species by Means of Natural Selection, or the Preservation of Favoured Races in the Struggle for Life* (1859/1982). So every white institution, called by whites euphemistically as "mainstream," sought to construct a way to maintain a system that had been "baked" from the beginning. The 20th century was the era of the motion picture, and it revolutionized images and sustained comfortable myths that allowed whites to see themselves as victors over the indigenous people as well as Africans. Teaching the lessons of conquest were preachers, professors, merchants, mechanics and engineers, and ordinary workers, hardly an inch above black people economically but cuddled by the system of white racial domination with the blanket of invincibility. Even when the Alsatian missionary Albert Schweitzer went on a medical mission to Gabon, it was in the interest of the spread of white superiority. Indeed, Chinua Achebe (1988/2012) was right to criticize the arrogance of Schweitzer, who felt himself superior to the Africans and essentially built his own plantation in the Gabonese forest, where he claimed, "Yes, the African is my brother, but my junior brother." Achebe does not only attack Schweitzer but also sees in Joseph Conrad some of the same racial arrogance. Indeed, Conrad, he says, portrays Africa as the "other world," meaning that it is the antithesis of Western civilization. What Achebe knows is that Europe sees itself as the superior civilization, and all of its popular and social history underwrites the cultural loan. There is an animus toward African people that Achebe can feel and sense in its most critical dimension. Hence, he quotes a passage from Conrad about his first encounter with an African: "A certain enormous buck nigger encountered in Haiti fixed my conception of blind, furious, unreasoning rage, as manifested in the human animal to the end of my days. Of the nigger I used to dream for years afterwards" (p. 9).

One can now understand how popular culture could promote this propaganda as an alternative reality in the world. Ideas such as racial purity and racial superiority became the material for popular consumption. Popular culture refers to the tastes and habits of ordinary people who have been influenced by the makers of opinion, the creators of artistic forms, and the engineers of social pleasures as found in entertainment, fashion, sports, videos, television, music, technology, and even politics. For a genre to be accepted as popular, it must find acceptance among the masses of society. Therefore, when we examine the relationship of race to popular culture, we are looking at the way race and racism factor into the making of drama, films, poetry, literature, video games, and music, and even infiltrate the workplace and the university. Nothing is left clean in the society; no one is left unaffected, although there are those who speak of unconscious bias, which is another way of saying that white racial domination has become unnoticeable to white people, who practice it as normal. Of course, there is enough in the society to suggest that this virus of race can and does affect black people as well. One of the best examples of this effect is the response to *A Soldier's Play* by Charles Fuller.

Fuller's *A Soldier's Play* won the Pulitzer Prize in 1982 and set popular culture in the United States on a truly multidimensional path. It is now recognized as a classic of courageous writing and human advocacy prior to the era of BLM. Fuller brought a powerful understanding beyond the commonplaces of race. He was able to see the nuances in humanity and, consequently, to see how the popular racial associations had to be changed to save African people. Some people misread his play, and in their misreading, they turned the play into a target for many disgruntled race proponents. Douglas Turner Ward, founder of the Negro Ensemble Company, who gave the play its first opening, held similar attitudes about human nature as those revealed in Fuller's complex play.

Fuller was the first of his generation, and probably the first of any American generation, to thoroughly tackle the issue of race as a farce. He knew almost from the beginning that it was a construction meant to entrap darker human beings in an endless trap of fighting to climb the racial ladder. Fuller taught us how to abandon race as a predictable instrument, although there were numerous people ready to pick it up once he dropped it, and he created a philosophical whirlwind that remains in our society. What was truly transformative in Fuller's mind was the fact that black people did not have to be button-holed into any particular category. The attendant idea seemed correct as well; whites did not have to be presumed to be always one way in their response to social situations. Fuller understood that it was difficult to think outside of the box of race that we had been accustomed to seeing and experiencing in the United States, Britain, France, and other white-dominated places. Yet he saw possibilities that were multidimensional.

The story seems straightforward enough at first glance. A soldier, Sergeant Vernon Waters, has been murdered on a racially segregated military base in Louisiana, in the American South. The U.S. Army has sent a highly ranked African American investigator, Richard Davenport, from Washington, D.C., to this relatively isolated army base in the 1940s to investigate the killing. One immediately gets the picture that the investigator was an unknown but welcome factor in the situation as far as the black troops were concerned. Of course, white officers who were the real commanders of these black troops were not so pleased to have a black investigator whose rank was equal to theirs, a typical racial reaction in the South at the time. The ranking white officer began immediately to express his dislike for the educated, sophisticated Harvard University–trained lawyer. No one on the military base had ever seen a highly ranked black officer. Davenport's only concern was "Who could have murdered a black sergeant on a military base in the South in 1944 during World War II?"

As in so many communities in the America of the 1940s, the situation on the military base reflected the bizarre "racial" climate one would have found outside the base. It was clear, once the investigator began to explore the situation, that the army regiment and surrounding countryside were boiling cauldrons of racial distrust. However, something not quite so obvious began to unfold as the investigator got deeper into the story. Vulnerabilities emerged around the idea of race in a racist country. In effect, Fuller rescues his readers from all of the entanglements of race that he has constructed in the play and shows how our vulnerabilities might point to a conclusion unlike our expectations.

Fuller had demonstrated since the time of his youth in Philadelphia the love of words, signs, and symbols embracing African American culture in a genuine way. Yet he does not permit an escape into the mysterious idealization of black people. His people are rounded, not singularly unproblematic, and they do things that all humans do; this is Fuller's main theme, which is a human meme. We have argued that centering Africans in narratives as agents is a significant achievement in a society that creates disconnects between the standard portrayal of reality and ordinary experiences. A black person who lives in the United States is often compelled to handle several contradictory relationships with the state, the local government, the overarching techno-structural realities of institutions and belief systems, and the hypocrisy of the keepers of the founding documents. How you keep sane in the midst of so much chaos is through mental discipline and a tough stance toward one's own sense of self. It is at once a statement and a narration of the centrality of African American experiences in the creation of human relationships.

One can actually see why Fuller would refuse to create predictable and idealized black characters. His characters love, laugh, and kill just like any human. This revelation was the linear stab wound into the flesh of racial perfectibility. Humans are flawed, and humans react to and are affected by the false notion of white supremacy in numerous intended and unintended ways. Black people have all the emotions and values that are found in any people; that is the real victory of Fuller's insight, and it is what has made him one of the most important writers of his times. There were those opposing writers who rejected the idea that a black man would be murdered by a black, particularly in the South on a racially segregated military base in the 1940s! The play shows through powerful portrayals the effects of racism on African Americans' self-concept, respect for African culture, and ultimately ideological and philosophical differences about how to deal with the complexity of racial domination. Fuller never loses sight of the popular culture, that is, the artificial framing of the race issue in the society.

There is no delusion here; there is only a false illusion created by the vast scaffolding of racism under which black people live and learn sometimes to dislike African culture. Self-hatred under oppression, Fuller tells us, can be quite natural. For some readers of the play, the assumption might be that the murderer has to be white; after all, the action takes place in a racist society where the killing of black men, especially black soldiers in uniform, was not unheard of in the South. However, Fuller launches into the psychology of intrablack relationships, honor, shame, expectations, self-hatred, and pride to eventually solve the murder.

The enduring quality of Fuller's thought derives from the judicious presentation of history with the ongoing problems of the present. The play shows us memory and magic, tension and laughter, discrimination and warfare, masculinity and caste. Weaving a story of men seeking to go to war and already at war with themselves, Fuller strips the phantasmagoric from black men and infuses them with the common humanity that exists where humans are free of the history and memory of racism and when they refuse to be cast in a vise of masculinity that ties them to the bigotry of the southern patriarchy. They were men, free men, black men, capable of anything, including murder. Who has not thought that black people in the United States, should the imagination be allowed to be free, could take up arms against the enemies of the people as other humans have done in other parts of the world? What keeps humans who are dark in check? The genius of *A Soldier's Story* is that it carries a theme that emanates from Fuller's fascination with the military and African American history yet he uses his intelligence and understanding of human beings to develop mature characters that are attached to motivating ideas.

Fuller sees humanity's condition clearly, although the play is not about whether racism exists or not; he knows that it is a reality of American life, but what he establishes with his characters, and the point of this narrative, is that African Americans, even with a rich and tolerant culture, soulful and liberated, can kill someone, a black man, in the era of segregation in the deepest, most ignorant part of the American apartheid empire. The trite conclusion would have been that the black man was killed by a white man since so many blacks had been lynched and mutilated in the South. That story had already been told a thousand times.

In recent years, the use of race to gain political influence, as in the case of Donald Trump, creates a massive problem with distortion, madness, and cowardly conversations. We must have the courage to speak the truth about the use of race to promote political power. Separation of people by race, especially where the propagandist shouts triumphally about his people who will stand with him regardless of his behavior, presents a democracy with a serious rift in how societies are bound together. Yet there is no doubt that a demagogue, using race as a theme, and his race as the favorite, might incite "his people" to insurrection, sedition, and even other forms of violence. Trump was a demagogue who had approached during his administration the status of a demigod, something he seemed to cherish as he watched his supporters storming the U.S. Capitol building on January 6, 2021.

Johnetta Betsch Cole (2021) writes in *Racism in American Public Life* that overcoming the propaganda about race to have a productive conversation means that we must admit certain facts. One, it is impossible to omit a discussion of the enslavement of Africans and believe that you can have an open conversation. She puts it this way: "First, any meaningful conversation about race and racism in America must include an acknowledgment of enslavement" (p. 48). She also argues that such a conversation about race must include a discussion about white skin privilege, which is heavily promoted in all public institutions. The real problem about race and racism in American culture is that it has been interwoven by every authority in the country, from the presidency to the local preachers in the country churches in Mississippi. Nevertheless, we have pushed back on the promoters of racism and now must push back further to attack the idea of race itself (Jaimes,1994). What is promoted in the popular media and social media are often caricatures of African people, some of which are self-created to be sure; however, the actions of the oppressed are often copied from their oppressors, and it is only in the radically innovative and bold actions of individuals such as LeBron James, Muhammad Ali, and Jackie Robinson, and hundreds of others, that we see real strength and courage to risk their millions to attack insane racism. Colin Kaepernick risked his entire professional football career to stand up for something; he is in the best tradition of the fighters against the framing of white domination over black people. Kaepernick's example will stand alongside the greatest feats of our men and women who have given their voices to social, political, and economic liberation from racism. Our history is replete with men and women who have defied the popular promotion of antiblack racism, from Maria Stewart to Angela Davis, from Diane Nash to Melina Abdullah. America has not been devoid of courageous African people who have introduced every conceivable argument to demonstrate the irrationality of white racism. In fact, the arguments have been made in the arts by Jesse Williams, Nina Simone, Sam Cooke, and Spike Lee; in athletics by James, Kaepernick, and Ali, among others; and in the academy by Maulana Karenga, Cornel West, Vivian Gordon, and Shirley Weber. What we are saying is that there is no shortage of Africans who have understood the problem of white racism and have shown true combat skills in every sector of society.

In Cole's wonderful book, she has a chapter titled "Imagine Our Nation Without Racism." There is something sad about that title for it relates to the history of African Americans who have fought in every corner and sector of the society to abolish racism. The fact is that one cannot imagine a nation, especially this nation, without racism. No, we are not expressing a dystopian view of relationships forever in America; we are staking our claim on something quite different in this discourse. After examining all of the social and political promotion of racism, white exceptionalism, perceptions of Africans as inferiors, and the rampant demagoguery around white nationalism, and the African American pushback in education, law, politics, religion, and economics in every conceivable way, it is clear to us that race must be eliminated to destroy racism. Indeed, we call for the reexamination of the African principles of Ma'at as an Afrocentric perspective on the divisions that Europe since the 17th century has encumbered us with in racist societies. Of course, as we have shown, this is not just a problem of Europeans, but as Paul C. Taylor (1988) has said quite well,

> It's just that after the seventeenth century or so, Europeans developed a vocabulary that highlights certain aspects of this process. And they didn't just develop this vocabulary. They refined it, exported it, tried to make it scientific, and built it into the foundation of world-shaping—world historical, Marx would say—developments in political economy. (p. 19)

The popular movies and videos especially showed ideas of white superiority with phantasmagoric images of other people in deference to the stability of white dignity and uprightness. Europeans introduced the race ladder in every land they entered in the era of European exploration. Neither Africans nor the indigenous people of the Americas had the concept of race. Prior to interacting with Europeans, the indigenous people of the Americas had no concept of race that could be used in the way the Europeans used the racial ladder (Jefferson, 1785/1995; Magnis, 1999). Hence, in popular media, the race meme took on a life of its own among the common people. Sadly, even the victims of this bizarre social contraption succumbed to its power as Native Americans and Africans were forced to learn the language of inferiority, something unknown in their ancient cultures. It is the same situation in Australia, where English has dominated and eliminated many ancient languages. There is now a movement to keep alive Miriwoong, a language that might go back more than 40,000 years; yet there are some who believe that this is a lost cause because it is a language spoken by people who have been degraded since the arrival of the English.

Although other Western nations certainly had their share of racist propaganda, especially the United Kingdom, Germany, France, and the Netherlands, it was the United States that assumed leadership in the popular images of race and the projection of racism during the 19th and 20th centuries. From the earlier founding Constitution of the United States in 1789, one sees the advancement of the idea of whites as different from other humans.

The First Nations communities were decimated in the Caribbean and on the two American continents in the quest for European expansion. Nevertheless, it was the relentless attacks on the history, psychology, and sociology of African people that made the European American the vanguard of white supremacy as a doctrine. It should now be clear that we are not arguing that one does not see physical difference in humans or that one cannot identify one language from another; rather, our position is that neither Africans nor indigenous people saw difference as reflective of superiority or inferiority. Popular media was used to underscore the legal existence of the inferiority of black people and the superiority of white people, in newspaper cartoons, on television, in the movies, and increasingly on social media platforms, despite the fact that there has always been rational and consistent pushback.

The Troubled History of Law and Popular Culture

Nearly 70 years after the establishment of the U.S. Constitution, a Supreme Court opinion written by Chief Justice Roger Taney in *Dred Scott v. Sandford* (1856) stated that the Constitution regarded blacks as "so far inferior that they had no rights which the white man was bound to respect, and that the negro might justly and lawfully be reduced to slavery for his benefit." Thus, the racial ladder was itself engraved in the mind of the chief justice of the U.S. Supreme Court. One can see, with some detours, a straight line from this claim by Taney to the treatment of black people like Brionna Taylor, Jacob Blake, and George Floyd by officers of the law. Thus, the troubled history of American law as the model for other instruments of narrative power in the country has instituted a line of thinking that calls for a counternarrative of a common humanity. To alter the criminal story against humanity, however, we must overcome the negation of blackness. The prosecution of this line of argument minimizes the notion of separate human capabilities based simply on biology.

Sometimes it is claimed that since race and color were not mentioned in the Declaration and Constitution it meant that the founding principles of the nation did not see color or establish race. This is not exactly the case since the social contract, the compact of government, did not include First Nations or African people. It was, as we have seen throughout history, a contract that white men made between themselves, and for it to extend to us, there would have to be those who looked at the Constitution and sought amendments and interpretations that spoke to racist policies and behaviors. In its founding, we know that the Constitution spoke of citizens and "other persons," a euphemism used for Africans and Indians, "not taxed" and in separate categories from citizens, who were white men. However, by the Fifteenth Amendment, race and color were written into the document itself in regard to the right to vote. Already, the Thirteenth Amendment had freed the enslaved Africans, and the Fourteenth Amendment had made Africans citizens, but the Fifteenth Amendment made it clear that voting was a right for all male citizens; it would have to be amended again. While it is true that James Madison remarked during the Philadelphia Constitutional Convention that it was "wrong to admit in the Constitution the idea that there could be property in men," the conventioneers used the euphemism "other people" several times. Of course, the founders sat in conference while several of them were major holders of enslaved Africans. Consider the amendments to the Constitution that came as the nation evolved and sought to correct the inherent problems in the founding document.

Amendments

The Thirteenth Amendment freed the enslaved Africans. This amendment was passed on January 31, 1865, and it abolished slavery and involuntary servitude, except as punishment for a crime. The amendment was ratified by 27 of the then 36 states on December 6, 1865, and proclaimed on December 18, 1865.

The Fourteenth Amendment gave Africans the right to citizenship and was adopted on July 9, 1868, as one of the Reconstruction Amendments. The amendment made Africans citizens and promised them equal protection under the law.

The Fifteenth Amendment established the right for African men to vote while also prohibiting states from denying a citizen the right to vote based on that citizen's "race, color, or previous condition of servitude." It was ratified on February 3, 1870.

Although these Amendments to the U.S. Constitutions were meant to change the status of Africans, they nevertheless enshrined a special, separate treatment for African people that has become a part of the popular perception of African people in the United States. After generations of Africans had been held in bondage, the writing of the amendments would have to compete with the already ingrained attitude found in American communities from the 17th century that blacks were inferior beings. Indeed, it was clearly retold in the language of some of the most important white Americans of the day. Jefferson clearly stated that "blacks are inferior to whites in the endowments of both body and mind."

Our point is that Jefferson's attitude, long before the amendments to the Constitution, was circulating in the minds of the brightest white men of that generation. One could conceive of a long chain of thoughts grounded and held together by popular belief that had been created decades before Jefferson; he was just the inheritor of such bad ideas about black people. Thus, it was the intention of the amendments to free the Africans, give them citizenship, and provide the right to vote, but in reality, states could and did, without equal protection under the law, discriminate against Africans and administer the law with an unequal hand. We claim that this practice of discrimination is related to the perception of Africans as inferior humans.

Our objective in this chapter is not to bring the American Constitution to the bar but rather to show that at the core of the most troubling debates about race and racism, whether it is affirmative action, police brutality, or aggressive incarceration of black people, the laws often follow the beliefs of the ruling folk. To defeat racial discrimination, we must be willing to root out the actions, the policies as Ibram Kendi says, and the popular uses of the racial ladder that are associated with racial animosities and perceptions. Consequently, the road from laws and policies to popular culture and social rhetoric is quite straightforward and very short. We have found that as the U.S. Congress was passing the three so-called Reconstruction Amendments to the Constitution, the popular theatrical actors were firing up the imaginations of the ordinary white masses with negative and cartoonish images of African people in the creation of minstrel shows.

The Racist's Urge

Minstrelsy is generally underrated in the creation of the popular culture against Africans because many white people assumed that it showed black people to be innocent, playful, and musical, qualities that they would have said at the time affirmed the humanity of African people, although they would say that their own traits were different—better, more rational, and correct. In fact, minstrelsy, a form of entertainment developed in the early 19th century, demonstrated the immense negativity that white people held about Africans. It was not endearment but ridicule that became the most important aspect of minstrelsy by the 1850s.

The minstrel show lampooned African people as stupid, slow-witted, buffoonish, superstitious, and lazy despite all of the evidence around them that the economy of the United States depended on the efficient and hard labor of Africans, the ingenuity of African inventors, and the thousands of serious attempts at escaping from bondage carried out by Africans. As an art form, the shows consisted of a variety of comic acts and dancing and musical performances. White actors dressed up in blackface pranced around on the stage playing the role of African people. A few Africans were often incorporated in the shows, but the superstars were usually whites who lampooned black people as lazy and foolish.

From the 1830s to the end of the Reconstruction, the minstrel shows were the main art shows in the American state. It had become an American national art form used to ease white audiences into opera and other European genres. Therefore, it was no wonder that the society would produce one of its most notorious examples of art serving the interests of racial doctrine at the beginning of the 20th century.

The Birth of a Nation

In 1915, as the minstrel period was waning, an American moviemaker, D. W. Griffith, made a silent epic, *Birth of a Nation*, based on Thomas Dixon Jr.'s novel called *The Clansman*, which drank from the dirtiest, crudest, and most racist pool of tropes in the American nation. Hailed as a historical landmark in film history, the film was three hours long and mixed history with fiction in an imaginative manner that made it a commercial success but set back racial attitudes for decades. It starts with John Wilkes Booth's assassination of Abraham Lincoln and chronicles the relationship of two families during the Civil War. In the movie, the Union family is called the Stonemans, and the Confederate family is called the Camerons.

There are two general characteristics of the movie: (1) its steeply racist narrative and (2) its introduction of cinematic innovations. The racist character of the film was its main point, but it is unfortunate that the powerful cinematic innovations were used to carve a hole into the American psyche that swallowed up Griffith's talents as it ensured a continuation of the negation of blackness. In fact, the introduction of close-up shots, fade-outs, a musical score for the film, an intermission, and scores of extras for the battle scenes was considered innovative, but these artistic contributions underscored a racist mythology. Even President Woodrow Wilson, himself a known racist, granted a viewing of the motion picture at the White House.

Birth of a Nation celebrated the rise of the Ku Klux Klan (KKK) in big-screen cinematic majesty; that was to be repeated 19 years later when Leni Riefenstahl's *Triumph of the Will*, a celebratory documentary of the Nazi regime, was both acclaimed and criticized because she used her skills to glorify the Nazi machine. Although the *kuklos*, the KKK circle, had waned around the turn of the century, Griffith's film gave it new life, and the anti-African organization set about using *Birth of the Nation* as a recruiting instrument, reinforcing the racist ideology in the white American masses. One of the lingering tropes was the sexually aggressive and unintelligent black man seeking to rape white women. Griffith depicts the KKK as a heroic cadre of white men protecting white women and preserving white supremacist behavior.

African Americans called on history and their courage to protest in the thousands against the film because of its incitement to violence and its vile portrayal of black men and women. The National Association for the Advancement of Colored People led the campaign to get the film banned, to no real effect on the popularity of the film among the whites. Indeed, the film did assist in making this organization a champion of African American indignation, resistance, and legal campaigns against blatantly racist policies.

Since the early 20th century, the rise of visual rhetoric, not merely the language spoken or written by propagandists but the actual use of visual images to reproduce propaganda about race, has become a formidable enforcer of the so-called natural order of racial hierarchy. We know from our own experiences that movies, television programs, and videos are all formed out of the historical elements in our societies. Only by changing reality can we truly have influence on what is produced. Art in its essence is the creation of those who have attempted to make the world see differently, but it is always out of the artist's vision that cultural meaning is attached to the creation. We are not saying that movies, for example, provide what is real but rather the reinvention of realities. Yet these reinventions in a racist society are bound to produce forms of the racial hierarchy even in a futuristic movie.

Given such a creative environment, that is, one where we are racialized by the assignations of the racial ladder, we often see a grotesque acceptance of superior and inferior places in the society. In other words, the racist structure, with its instructions, has dictated what is to be accepted by the people who are classified by the racial ladder. It is easy to see how Frantz Fanon, as a young man trying to make sense of the world into which he had been born, could be appalled by the epithet "dirty nigger" hurled at him by those who called themselves whites. Neither he nor his people had participated in this racialization process, yet he was a victim of it in the popular and academic media. In most instances, Africans had very little to do with the nature of the society. Whites could, at will, change the laws and regulations to benefit themselves. In a pattern that has been repeated in American history, when white supremacy as a doctrine cannot exist, those in charge seek to change the rules. Let us look at the record of the medical profession at the turn of the century.

The Role of Medicine

Often because of the race paradigm, we have seen the insistence on the part of racists in history that whatever is practiced by black people must be questioned, sanctioned, and sometimes destroyed. Nothing illustrates this more than the *Abraham Flexner Report* of 1910. Forty-five years earlier, nearly 4 million Africans had been enslaved, and in 1910, nearly 9 million Africans lived in the United States. An enterprising people built colleges, churches, banks, and even hospitals to rise quickly from slavery.

During the enslavement, the health of black people was largely the responsibility of African healers on the plantations, although always with the oversight of the white slaveholders, who held a commercial interest in every black person's body. A few black healers at the beginning of the 20th century, like Plenty Smith, of Dooly County, Georgia, became famous for taking care of black and white patients. Gifted with knowledge of herbs and roots, some of these doctors were called root doctors, experts in the use of plants to heal various ailments. However, by the turn of the century, there was enough concern among white people about unregulated medicine, especially since many of the midwives were African Americans, that white doctors thought that medicine should be regulated.

When regulations happened, of course, many black doctors and midwives could no longer perform their work. In effect, regulation stripped authority from medicine people who were untrained by schools. Black people were free to practice medicine until the appearance of the Flexner Report. While during the enslavement, Africans were used for medical experimentation and black bodies regularly experimented on, the era of freedom after the Civil War saw black medical schools and colleges. However, it is widely known that several decades later the infamous syphilis experiment would be carried out on black men in Alabama (Gray, 2002; Jones, 1993). The impact of this experiment is often cited as one of the reasons African Americans refused to take the coronavirus vaccinations at the same rate as white America. Racialized medicine and unequal treatment had poisoned the well of trust, turning it into a pool of distrust.

As chattels during the enslavement, Africans had no rights and did not own their bodies. The slaveholders gave consent for surgeries and other medical procedures on the Africans they held. The whites performing the procedures would be given food and lodging while they were carrying out their work of practicing on black people (Bankole, 1998).

In 1904, the president of the Council of Medical Education and the American Medical Association hired Abraham Flexner, a schoolmaster, to travel to 155 medical schools and make evaluations of their practices. When Flexner's report came out, it had an immense impact on medical education in the African American community, closing down the majority of the black medical schools but suggesting that it might be good for blacks to treat other blacks (Flexner & Pritchett, 1910).

Flexner found most black medical practitioners inadequate, and many of the most effective doctors lost their right to practice. What this tells us is that medical racism against African people existed during the enslavement and affected the men and women of medical science in the 20th century.

In 1951, a young African American mother of five, Henrietta Lacks, went to the hospital at Johns Hopkins to be treated for cervical cancer. Lacks died on October 4, 1951, and cells taken from her have continued to be used for scientific research. Given the name HeLa, for her two names Henrietta and Lacks, this cell line is immortal. Her cells kept on reproducing when most cells would die. The cells were taken from her on February 8, 1951, and since that time, her cells have been used in research by thousands of laboratories around the world. Her family were not immediately told about the use of her cells for science, and once it was discovered, they saw this as yet another example of the medical exploitation of the African person. It took years before the U.S. government and Johns Hopkins were able to come to terms with the family.

Surely the entire pantheon of Western scholars are not practicing racism, but some live within the confines of the race paradigm, and that in itself makes it difficult for most escape. There are notable examples of ideological and theoretical experimenters seeking to detach themselves from the worst aspects of Western culture. Race delivers strange and bizarre characters who parade across the stage of humanity afflicted with the worst handicaps of a people whose narcissistic minds have entrapped them in their own images. Karl Marx and Vladimir Lenin could not see Africa or Africans. Martin Heidegger toyed with the ideology of the Nazis, hooked as he was like René Schwaller de Lubicz, who was blind to the African origin of the consciousness he sought among the columns of Luxor along the Nile. Jean-Paul Sartre tried hard to assert the value of an antiracist racism in support of Negritude, and yet the sum total of the endeavors of Europe's brightest minds amounts to almost nothing in stemming the promotion of the racial ladder. This is not to say that thinkers did not try; a few did, and some recognized the problematics found in Western culture when it came to ideas of modernity and even postmodernity. A few European writers of the 20th and 21st centuries have tried to break out of the box into which they were born. After the Hitlerian terror of the Second International European War (often called World War II), when the Nazis unleashed the holocaust against the Jewish and Roma people, invaded the vast Russian plains, and overturned democracies in Europe, a bevy of European thinkers, stunned by the insanity and barbarity of the

Third Reich's promotion and prosecution of hate and madness, arose from the ashes to discover points of light everywhere they could. Among these thinkers were people such as Michel Foucault and Jacques Derrida. They could hardly have been any more different in their responses to what they saw as the utter descent into irrationality brought about by the European war. In Foucault's case he seemed to have entered into a pact with the past that allowed him the freedom to tinker with the worst tendencies of the Western paradigm, not to bring it down but to reform its worst elements. While it is easy for us as Africologists to see why Foucault would be disheartened by the Western treatment of the "other," we also see this problem as one deeply entrenched in the way Europe and America have thought of people, of humanity.

For his part, Foucault sought a new, more sensitive way of approaching human failings. The breakdown of institutions in Europe because of the vile, rambunctious, racist, and antisemitic notions of Adolf Hitler had chastened the doctrine of white supremacy and had shown the entire world what a German-directed racial ideology could do to Europe and to the rest of the world. Hitler's brazen attempt at domination was shocking to Foucault and others because Hitler did not simply build on Europe's domination of people in Africa, Asia, and South America; he literally overran countries in Europe itself. Consequently, Foucault saw how power and knowledge combined in a vise of social control and influence of various institutions. At times toying with the idea of becoming a Marxist or at least a Hegelian, he abandoned any thought of being an active follower of either idea but ended up anyway taking hold of the ideas of structuralism. We can think of him as a structuralist with postmodernist tendencies, like Jacques Lacan, Roland Barthes, Claude Lévi-Strauss, and others who sought to counter the existentialism of Sartre. However, Foucault's book *The Order of Things* (1966/1989) championed the idea that certain conditions have always existed for what was considered acceptable in society as truth in a scientific sense. Rejecting Marxism as being tied to the 19th century, Foucault joined the antistructuralists, proclaiming that European philosophy must adopt a new orientation.

In the book *Mental Illness and Personality* (1954), Foucault had demonstrated that in actuality he was an eclectic who combined all theories and philosophies to assist him in understanding the nature of life. His book *Madness and Civilization: A History of Insanity in the Age of Reason* (1961/1988) thrust him into the forefront of the discourses in psychology, politics, and literary criticism, although he said little about race. The hardcore problem was the fact that Foucault did not deal with race or racism, although in France and other parts of Europe the population of Africans was increasing daily. His studies of European cultures helped us understand the difficulties with the systems that controlled the lives of the poor and helpless. One knows that had he studied disciplinary institutions with attention to the treatment of non-Europeans he would have found abuse all around. In fact, one can assume that had there been an American Foucault the prison system itself would have revealed the disparate treatment of prisoners based on the race paradigm. This situation would have been compounded had he examined the asylums and manufacturing floors. Later, in his books *Discipline and Punish* (1975/1995) and *History of Madness* (2009), he studied the othering of insane people and then got involved in speaking against persecutions, social segregation, and anti-Semitism, which had not been on his radar as a younger thinker. So it is possible to claim that Foucault was on the road to freedom from the entanglements of the racial box.

In the years after the rise of Foucault, the emergence of numerous European thinkers affected by the war and the rupture of structure gave birth to a generation of fierce antistructuralists. Among these thinkers was Derrida, who was born in Algeria in a Sephardic Jewish family in 1930. At 12 years, he was expelled from his school because of the anti-Jewish policy of France's Vichy government, which had imposed a quota on Jews. Derrida started reading philosophy, especially the works of Jean-Jacques Rousseau, Friedrich Nietzsche, Albert Camus, and Jean-Paul

Sartre, and moved to Paris after the war in 1949. He would also become a familiar lecturer in American universities. In the late 1960s, he published *Writing and Difference* (1967c), *Speech and Phenomena* (1967b), and *Of Grammatology* (1967a). Probably influenced by the movement for civil rights and Black Power in the United States, Derrida soon found his footing on the issue of race. In "Racism's Last Words," Derrida (1985) says, "Even though it offers the excuse of blood, color, birth—or, rather, because it uses this naturalist and sometimes creationist discourse—racism always betrays the perversion of a man, the 'talking animal'" (p. 4). He further argues, "It institutes, declares, writes, inscribes, prescribes. A system of marks, it outlines space in order to assign forced residence or to close off borders. It does not discern, it discriminates" (p. 4).

Derrida saw the assault on reason and values in the preceding decades and sought to demonstrate the limits of what had been constructed by the structuralists. Indeed, his emphasis on deconstruction is a subversion of the binary oppositions found in the dominant thinking of Western culture—this notion of speech/writing, presence/absence, dark/light, and so forth. Fluidity is a value much unlike the idea of that which is stable and solid. Derrida (1985) comes at these points from both philosophical and literary directions as he wonders what South Africa would be without apartheid. Thus, he says,

> This new satellite of humanity, then, will move from place to place, it too, like a mobile and stable habitat, "mobile" and "stabile," a place of observation, information, and witness. A satellite is a guard, it keeps watch and gives warning: Do not forget apartheid, save humanity from this evil, an evil that cannot be summed up in the principial and abstract iniquity of a system. It is also daily suffering, oppression, poverty, violence, torture inflicted by an arrogant white minority (16% of the population, controlling 60% to 65% of the national revenue) on the mass of the black population. (p. 5).

Perhaps it is Boaventura de Sousa Santos, who was born on November 15, 1940, in Coimbra, Portugal, and studied at Coimbra, Berlin, and Yale, who has captured the imagination of many progressives in the Western world for his insistence on looking to the south. Indeed, Molefi Kete Asante's book *Facing South to Africa* (2014) appears to be in title a rift from Sousa Santos's concerns in *Epistemologies of the South: Justice Against Epistemicide* (2014). In the book *The End of the Cognitive Empire* (2018), Sousa Santos enlarged his views, expanding his attacks on the same institutions that had been questioned by Foucault and to some extent Derrida. However, it was his intellectual activism around the civil rights movement, the movement for Black Power, and the anti–Vietnam war movement that drove him toward a reconceptualization of the Western epistemology. Nevertheless, this valiant attempt, in ways similar to that of Noam Chomsky, pitted Sousa Santos against less progressive Western intellectuals who saw him catering to the south. Yet Chomsky, although considerably anti-establishment, did not see Marxism as the way forward for the European project in the way that Sousa Santos was later to see it. Chomsky was attached to a different project, which might be called a libertarian socialism and anarcho-syndicalism. Chomsky's aim was to empower the syndicates of the workers, the unions, with the ability to abolish wage structures and impose worker control and influence on manufacturing and the society. In the view of the anarcho-syndicalists, workers would end wage slavery and impose self-management. In fact, Chomsky is the most convincing of the European American authors on the subject of race, especially in the United States, where he says white supremacy was more primitive, savage, and extreme than in South Africa. All major institutions in the United States were created or expanded by the oppression of African people who established the economic base for America. Cotton production was the basis for the financial and commercial system. Chomsky cites in an interview on Democracy Now (2015) Edward Baptiste's (2016) *The Half Has Never Been Told*, where the author points out that the plantation was nothing more than a slave labor camp where the bullwhip slave drivers forced workers to work to the point of death, working harder and harder to produce more produce or products than any other sector in society.

The Ignorance of Racial Perception

There have been incredibly ignorant moments in the lives of African people when whites ask questions like "Do the people of Africa live in houses?" "Are there languages in Africa?" "Do Africans have tails?" and various other questions indicating a severe form of racial indoctrination. If you are taught that black people are either subhuman or nonhuman, after a while, it becomes quite easy to see how black people can be brutalized and killed without much remorse.

One has to examine how the social construction of race, as we have discussed, is similar to the hierarchy of gender in order to understand how popular culture serves the interests of patriarchy and hierarchy. The codes of the racial system are written or portrayed in society's cultural channels and beamed or cabled to audiences who accept these codes as reality. It is no wonder that the system inherited in American society as racial hierarchy has worked regardless of who the leader, president, judges, or lawyers happened to be. The most socially liberal, thinking president of the United States will not be able to turn the cards on the racist system; it will have to be done by a series of movements to undo the classifications and assignations of race.

What has occurred during the first part of the 21st century is a strong and insistent movement of African Americans to tear down this social construct. This is the meaning of Black Lives Matter. A social construct is dead if the people for whom it is assigned no longer believe in it. There are also whites who have disavowed the idea of white superiority. The moment when 17-year-old Kyle Rittenhouse killed the white demonstrators Anthony Huber and Joseph Rosenbaum and injured Gaige Grosskreutz on August 25, 2020, galvanized the thinking of numerous white and black people who saw the shooting as a desperate effort to enforce the racial order. Like the 1964 Freedom Summer killing of James Chaney, Andrew Goodman, and Michael Schwerner, the deaths of Rosenbaum and Huber stood as signals to the system that it could no longer hold on to the social construct of race. It has been, as Martin Luther King Jr. once observed about segregation, on its deathbed, although the death notice has not been posted. Since the 1960s, there have been numerous documentary films that have described the persistence of racial animus toward African Americans. Fortunately, black filmmakers and others are taking to the genre with vigor to combat racist thinking.

Film is one of the most ideologically creative acts because it is developed with a script, a plot, and characters in a story web that tells us precisely the orientation of the filmmaker. Of course, the filmmaker is often a creature of systemic racism, that is, the racial ladder in American society. It is remarkable that Ta-Nehisi Coates, the popular writer, in an interview on MSNBC on August 29, 2020, stated that he did not see an end to the George Floyd–type killings of black men. Coates said, "It will happen again." One does not have to know anything about racism to know that the generator of racist actions and policies has an infinite way of expressing itself. This is precisely why Coates could think that it would never end. Of course, racism, racialism, and all their attendant characteristics are parts of the same quilt of circumstances made from the same fabric. They see Africans as less than white people and are willing to give whites an advantage in terms of expectations, promotions, benefit of doubt, prison sentencing, or privileges.

Joseph Feagin is a dominant antiracist thinker whose books and articles have been read and studied by numerous scholars. Feagin promoted the idea of racial framing and as a key social theorist conducted extensive research on racial and gender issues. The author of more than 70 books, Feagin's research provides us with a detailed understanding of the systemic critique of racial theories. Spending much of his life trying to clarify for others the complexities, intersections, and crises of the racial system in the United States, Feagin has studied microaggressions, language and racial analysis, and the global color line. Feagin (2020) considered racism as a part of the entire Western project because

> the rise of Western capitalism is rooted in the global seizing of the land, resources, and labor of people of color by violent means. Commercial and industrial capitalism develops over this era because of the expanding Atlantic system of slavery. (p. 14)

Out of Feagin's conceptual incubator have come other ideas about the nature of racism as it relates to the maintenance of the system of oppression and white privilege. Some have spoken of the idea of white privilege as a system imposed in a multicultural society, and others have seen the manufacture of common forms of white nationalism that occupy the interests of ordinary white people who are willing to follow the lead of those often referred to as "elite nationalists," whose hands are not necessarily shown when the ball is advanced to support the interests of privilege. It is what Feagin refers to as elite white male dominance at work in keeping homeostasis in the system by utilizing the fierce passions of the battalions of whites who feel that they are somehow better than blacks and other people. At the elite levels, this practice operates in the engendering of images, icons, and values that produce a population susceptible to the irrational idea that some human beings are better than others. It becomes a traditional meme difficult to root out of a system where the ground has been made fertile enough to receive it without resistance. One can see this in political circles, where those who use populist sentiments to subvert the economy, society, and unity of people for their own political purposes are simply buying into the social markets that they have set up themselves. In the United States, it was easy to see how Trump as president played the emotions of white people like a guitarist to his political advantage.

He saw himself not like the ordinary white people but as one of the elite white males who practiced their own form of domination, which means ultimately the subjugation of not just those not white but also whites who believed in a just and multicultural democracy. Feagin has pointed out so correctly in *Racist America* (2014) that the creators of the Constitution of the United States who met in Philadelphia were not seeking merely to create "a new bourgeois-democratic government; it was also a meeting to protect the racial and economic interests of [white] men with substantial wealth in the colonies" (p. 3). In fact, they used pamphlets, broadsides, and newspapers to further assert the popular doctrine that they had created a "republic," but it was certainly a republic deeply flawed with the racial virus. Neither black men nor black women would be brought into this colonial machine for the distribution of wealth and the pursuit of happiness. It would take years before the evolution of the society, through Civil War and protests and petitions, would cause it to bend a little and yield a view of what was possible in a society with equity, diversity, and justice. Our argument, however, is that the racial framing of the society that we find in the 19th and 20th centuries, and into the 21st century, has a history prior to the Constitution and has shown a resilience after the civil rights movement of the 1960s such that we can call it a normalization of racism. The pervasiveness of the racial ideology means that some whites see it as normal for whites to exercise their privilege to the disadvantage of blacks because in their minds black people are inferior in every respect. How could such an idea take hold in society without the participation of the principals, and as we have seen, all the way up to the presidency? As Feagin (2014) saw it, the framers of the Constitution had begun to legitimize "a system of racial oppression that they thought would ensure that whites, especially men of means, would rule for centuries" (p. 46). Robert Parkinson wrote in *The Common Cause: Creating Race and Nation in the American Revolution* (2016) that the framers of the Constitution used their white racism even in their military engagement with the British. In

1782, Benjamin Franklin, according to Parkinson, devised a scheme to ensure that Britain and the colonies would not reconcile. He said that American soldiers had found a bag with the scalps of women and children taken by the Seneca Indians. He then created a letter supposedly written by Naval Commander John Paul Jones urging independence because the king "engages savages to murder their defenseless farmers, women and children." Racism sat in the rooms with the founders as they created a nationalist ethos that helped in the formation of white fears of rebellious Africans and riotous indigenous people. The model for generating public distrust in other races and the highlighting of a patriot narrative that would drive white nationalism took their mold from the American founding gatherings.

Massaged into the public ethos was this extraordinary racial desire to maintain white domination in a country that had its own indigenous populations and hundreds of thousands of Africans marginalized on the periphery of human discourse. In effect, white people believed that they were neither savages nor barbarians despite the lethality of their lies about themselves and others. Ideas about hypocrisy multiplied in the minds and writings of African Americans who knew that the founding documents did not reflect the policies or behaviors of the people who claimed those documents as sacred.

Responding to Deep Media

The African American response to the rhetoric of white superiority and black inferiority in words, images, and actions has been varied: protests, soldier defections to other nations, self-hatred, emigration, and violent resistance. For 4 centuries, black people in the United States have used every instrument possible to break through the steel wall of racism in the media, whether written or moving. In most cases, protests have been the favorite strategy to combat the racial ladder and racial framing policies. A growing number of African Americans have chosen the option of leaving the United States for other nations. This has been a choice since enslaved Africans left the South for the North and then left the North for Canada in the 18th and 19th centuries. Leaving the source of oppression and brutality is one of the most natural actions to be taken by those who feel victimized. Black people in the United States have traveled to Mexico, Canada, or the Bahamas, and even as far away as Europe to escape the social conditions in America. At one time, France and the United Kingdom were two of the most attractive places for African American actors, artists, and musicians who believed, probably erroneously, that those countries were less victims of the racial ladder.

There were numerous defections of African American troops during almost every war fought by the United States. From the period of the Revolutionary War, when black people joined with the Loyalists who promised freedom and fought on the side of the British and then retreated with them to Halifax, Nova Scotia, to the hundreds of Africans who remained in Germany, France, Japan, Korea, and Vietnam as symbols of resistance to racism, African Americans have shown their distaste for white supremacist ideas. Thus, the defectors who were found in the two international European wars (called World Wars I and II), the American War in the Philippines, the Korean War, and the Vietnam War did not start a tradition; they simply believed that life could not be any worse for them than what they had seen in the United States. Notably, David Fagen gained international recognition for his leadership of guerilla forces during the time the Philippines was fighting for independence from the United States. Fagen, born in Tampa, Florida, joined the Army's segregated Twenty-Fourth Infantry Regiment in 1898 in Tampa as it prepared to fight in the Spanish-American War in Cuba. Run-ins with white southern officers meant that Fagen was given harsh punishment that could be considered among his reasons for deserting the American army at a time when lynchings of African Americans were at their highest point. It was not difficult for Fagen to see that racism was connected to colonialism. He rose to the rank of captain among the Filipinos and became a successful military leader.

Unfortunately, there are some Africans who accept the negativity that whites have articulated against blackness. They have become self-haters, believing that whites are superior and blacks are inferior; they have become victims of the negative popular cultural images. Negative images of oneself implicate the United States' white national and imperial racism. Yaba Blay's (2013) work *(1)ne Drop: Shifting the Lens on Race* allows the reader to see the extent of the horrible tragedy of Africans in a white supremacist culture despising their own appearance.

Perhaps a more subtle and nuanced response to white racial actions has been the silent emigration of Africans to countries in Africa and other parts of the world. In the book *The African American People: A Global History*, Asante (2011) showed that African Americans were found in Scandinavia and Japan to a greater degree than one would expect. Increasingly, since the dawn of African independence, thousands of Africans from the United States have moved to the African continent, especially to Ghana, South Africa, Zimbabwe, and Nigeria. Often receiving their retirement pensions and social security payments in African nations with lower living expenses, the émigrés find themselves in a less stressful environment than the United States. Canada has also become attractive for African American writers, poets, filmmakers, and novelists, much like the attraction of Paris and London during the 1960s and 1970s.

Given the almost endemic nature of the racial pandemic in the United States, it is almost miraculous that violent resistance has not taken a stronger pivot. Of course, there are reasons for this reluctance to resist on a large scale, although there have always been black people willing to take up arms in defense of their own homes and neighborhoods. There are two historical restraints that make active violence against white supremacists less likely. First, the African American community is heavily Christian, and the religion teaches obedience to earthly hierarchy. Second, African Americans often exhibit a historical idea of optimism stemming from the experiences of enslavement. Keeping hope alive even in the face of the most horrific terror was one way to survive the years of deprivation. One day, parents told children, the day will come when "all God's chillun' gon be free." Such incredible patience often stunts activism against the perpetrators of fear and hatred of African Americans. Yet there have been and are, from time to time, those who have assumed the stature of community defenders. With the unequal militarization of the black and white communities, those efforts have not been necessarily as effective as often predicted.

An entire quiver of responses will continue to be the African reaction to popular media's undermining of black people's dignity, rights, and history. As popular culture invents new avenues of attack through social platforms such as Facebook, Twitter, Instagram, and so forth, the African community will undoubtedly adopt more innovative forms of reaction. In the end, the assertion of a common humanity must be at the core of all positive responses to negative media. As Leland Melvin, the African American astronaut who wrote *Chasing Space* (2017) says, when you look at the earth from space, it is clear that we are one connected civilization. Africans were the first to know this fact because all of the people who left Africa to people other continents were Africans first, despite all popular media fronts that seek to deny the fact.

REFERENCES AND NOTES

Achebe, C. (2012). An image of Africa: Racism in Conrad's *Heart of Darkness*. In *Hopes and impediments: Selected essays*. Penguin. (Original work published 1988)

 This lecture was first given in 1975 at the University of Massachusetts–Amherst.

Asante, M. K. (2011). *The African American people: A global history*. Routledge.

 The African American People is the first book to take a global look at the role African Americans have played in the world. The book synthesizes the familiar tale of history's effect on the African people, who found themselves forced into enslavement and emerged as a world community.

Asante, M. K. (2014). *Facing south to Africa: Toward an Afrocentric critical orientation* (Critical Africana Studies). Lexington Books.

Bankole, K. K. (1998). *Slavery and medicine: Enslavement and medical practices in Antebellum Louisiana*. Garland.

Baptiste, E. (2016). *The half has never been told: Slavery and the making of American capitalism*. Basic Books.

Blay, Y. (2013). *(1)ne Drop: Shifting the lens on race*. Blackprint Press.

> Blay has taken on the issue of colorism as an extension of anti-black racism in the American society. By examining the nature of racism through the lens of black self-hatred, she shows the moral injury that has occurred in the African population. Beginning with the so-called one drop principle where any person with a hint of African ancestry is considered black and hence can be a victim of oppression in the United States, Blay seeks to correct this formulation by leaning in the direction of our main thesis about the elimination of race. One does not have to eliminate color to eliminate race, but by eliminating race, color becomes less important in our social lives.

Cole, J. B. (2021). *Racism in American public life: A call to action*. University of Virginia Press. https://doi.org/10.2307/j.ctv1bd4n09

> Cole provides the reader with an exceptional penetration into her public self to demonstrate the pervasive nature of racism. She argues that it is necessary for Americans to act to solve the problem caused by the racial virus.

Darwin, C. (1982). *On the origin of species by means of natural selection, or the preservation of favoured races in the struggle for life*. Penguin Books. https://doi.org/10.5962/bhl.title.68064 (Original work published 1859)

Democracy Now. (2015, March 3). *Noam Chomsky on Black Lives Matter: Why won't U.S. own up to history of slavery and racism?* [Video]. YouTube. https://www.youtube.com/watch?v=s-0BmqyWJ30

Derrida, J. (1967a). *Of grammatology* (G. C. Spivak, Trans.). Les Editions de Minuit.

Derrida, J. (1967b). *Speech and phenomena* (D. B. Allison, Trans.). Northwestern University Press.

Derrida, J. (1967c). *Writing and difference* (A. Bass, Trans.). University of Chicago Press.

Derrida, J. (1985). Racism's last word (P. Kamuf, Trans.). *Critical Inquiry, 12*(1), 290–300. https://doi.org/10.1086/448331

Dred Scott v. Sandford, 60 U.S. 393 (1856). https://supreme.justia.com/cases/federal/us/60/393/

Extratv. (2020, September 8). *Donald Trump Jr. on BLM, Jacob Blake, and Kyle Rittenhouse, plus: He explains "liberal privilege"* [Video]. YouTube. https://www.youtube.com/watch?v=IhQ0fLHT100

> The twice impeached president was one of the most unrestrained presidents in the history of the United States. His speeches, often bombastic attacks against everyone who was not white, became models of indecency against immigrants, the disabled, or people who were poor.

Feagin, J. R. (2014). *Racist America*. Routledge. https://doi.org/10.4324/9780203762370

    In this popular book, Feagin describes the reasons why the claims of a "racist" America are not only accurate but an admission that the society does not provide equal opportunities to African Americans.

Feagin, J. R. (2020). *The white racial frame: Centuries of racial framing and counter framing*. Routledge. https://doi.org/10.4324/9780429353246

    Feagin may be the most authoritative sociologist writing on race. He has advanced the theory of white racial framing to examine the ways racism, white racial domination, operates on a large scale in American society. His work is straightforward, clear, and teachable.

Flexner, A., & Pritchett, H. S. (1910). *Medical education in the United States and Canada: A report to the Carnegie Foundation for the Advancement of Teaching*. Carnegie Foundation for the Advancement of Teaching.

Foucault, M. (1954). *Mental illness and personality* (D. Eribon, Trans.). Macmillan.

Foucault, M. (1988). *Madness and civilization: A history of insanity in the age of reason*. Routledge. https://doi.org/10.4324/9780203278796 (Original work published 1961)

Foucault, M. (1989). *The order of things: An archaeology of the human sciences*. Routledge. (Original work published 1966)

Foucault, M. (1995). *Discipline and punish: The birth of the prison*. Vintage. (Original work published 1975)

Foucault, M. (2009). *History of madness*. Routledge.

Fuller, C. (1981). *A soldier's play*. Hill & Wang.

Gray, F. (2002). *The Tuskegee syphilis study: An insiders' account of the shocking medical experiment conducted by government doctors against African American men*. NewSouth Books.

Jaimes, M. A. (1994). American racism: The impact on American-Indian identity and survival. In S. Gregory & R. Sanjek (Eds.), *Race* (pp. 41–61). Rutgers University Press.

Jefferson, T. (1995). *Notes on the state of Virginia*. Penguin. (Original work published 1785)

    These notes, a series of letters and commentaries by Jefferson, announce his opinions on a variety of issues having to do with political and social relationships. They have been probed for his beliefs about race, democracy, and the necessity for continued vigilance.

Jones, J. H. (1993). *Bad blood: The Tuskegee syphilis experiment* (New and expanded ed.). Free Press.

Magnis, N. (1999). Thomas Jefferson and slavery: An analysis of his racist thinking as revealed by his writings and political behavior. *Journal of Black Studies, 29*(4), 491–509. https://doi.org/10.1177/002193479902900402

Obviously, as Magnis explains, Jefferson appears to have some dissonance between his writings and his actions. Not only did he hold several hundred Africans in bondage, but he also held opinions about the Africans' abilities that were disputed by people such as Benjamin Banneker. Nevertheless, he fathered children by Sally Hemings, a young woman of African ancestry.

McLuhan, M. (1966). *Understanding media*. Penguin.

Melvin, L. (2017). *Chasing space: An astronaut's story of grit, grace and second chances*. Amistad.

Melvin's story is like that of many African American men and women of science. They rise above the circumstances that have been created by "white" spaces to demonstrate, without seeking to stage demonstrations, that all humans have capabilities and the capacity for genius, distinction, and excellence is not reserved for whites.

MSNBC. (2020, August 29). *Ta-Nehisi: We must understand George Floyd, Breonna Taylor were human lives taken* [Video]. YouTube. https://www.youtube.com/watch?v=V6snowId-5Y

Parkinson, R. (2016). *The common cause: Creating race and nation in the American Revolution*. University of North Carolina Press. https://doi.org/10.5149/northcarolina/9781469626635.001.0001

Sousa Santos, B. de. (2014). *Epistemologies of the South: Justice against epistemicide*. Routledge.

This book was the first attempt by the author to challenge the reigning Eurocentric paradigm that included all of the crimes of brutality, sexism, rampant greed, and groupthink without intervention.

Sousa Santos, B. de. (2018). *The end of the cognitive empire: The coming of age of epistemologies of the South*. Duke University Press. https://doi.org/10.1215/9781478002000

The innovation in the author's thought is the audacious use of the South as a model of what is possible in a world without capital exploitation, patriarchy, and gender inequality.

Taylor, P. C. (1988). *Race: A philosophical introduction*. Polity Press.

In this book, Taylor defines various aspects and dimensions of the race idea to render it more accessible to those who seek to understand how it has come to dominate so much of Western thinking.

Towns, A. (2019). The (black) elephant in the room: McLuhan and the racial. *Canadian Journal of Communication, 44*(4), 545–554. https://doi.org/10.22230/cjc.2019v44n4a3721

A brilliant and original article that examines how Canada's major philosopher of communication treats the racial in his popular books.

CHAPTER 5

Beyond Race: The Quest Back to Humanity

During the January 6, 2021, insurrection, a white man being beaten by the mob of white terrorists at the Capitol building shouted at his angry attackers, "You are treating me like a black person." It reminded us of the case of the white doctor who complained to police at the Orlando International Airport in April 2018 that he "was being treated like a black person" (Ethan Sacks, August 17, 2018, *NBC News*). These are just two of the hundreds of thousands of cases of recognition by whites that to be treated like you were "black" is to be treated aggressively and often violently. Quite frankly, this is the result of the perception of whiteness as privileged and blackness as condemnation.

The sacred task of this generation is to unravel the conundrum of racial classification and to eradicate the vestiges of white delusions about a religious relationship to doctrines of white supremacy. It has taken centuries for whites to imagine, develop, and articulate the complex series of memes, symbols, arguments, and dog whistles to justify and promote the illusion of racial hierarchy. It is quite easy to see how this has emerged in the combination of faith and fiction.

Christian consciousness as interpreted in the period after the Crusades was racial in the idea of attaching color to inferiority or superiority. One can see from the 14th and 15th centuries that Europeans, particularly Portuguese and Castilians, were easily victimized by the papal bulls issued by the Roman pontiffs announcing their dominance over all non-Christians. In 1443, Eugenius IV issued *Rex regum* to show the church's neutrality in the Portuguese and Castilian disputes over African lands. The church entered to play the arbiter based on the inherited ideologies of black inferiority ingrained into the soil of Western society by the Hebraic ideologies related to Shem, Ham, and Japhet and the Islamic doctrines that saw Bilal, Muhammad's slave, as the model representative of the African people. By 1454, Pope Nicholas V had written to King Afonso V of Portugal confirming the Portuguese dominion over lands south of Cape Bojador in Africa. Encouraging the Portuguese to seize the lands of the Arabs and Turks and all other non-Christians, the *Romanus Pontifex*, as the papal bull was called, also gave permission for the enslavement of Africans, Saracens, and Turks. In effect, the pope's aim was to ensure that no other Western nation interfered with the rule and ascendancy of the Castilian and Portuguese powers.

One could see how the European diaspora across the globe would carry the spirit of white domination. In South Africa, the United States, Brazil, New Zealand, and Australia, and other lands where whites held dominion and political sway, they ramped up their assaults on the humanity of other people. The Germans in Namibia killed thousands of Herero people in one day, mowing them down with machine guns. In the southern Australian island of Tasmania, John Batman with cohorts of raiders hunted down Tasmanian people, killing them in their own lands. The Boers in South Africa often led troops like the Selous Scouts with the objective of killing every black person, man, woman, or child, as they made their way into the interior of Africa. In the Congo, King Leopold of Belgium, near the turn of the 20th century, allowed the brutal, cold-hearted, and murderous

Henry Morton Stanley and his *Force Publique* to maim and kill millions of Congolese in the pursuit of rubber.

By the 20th century, the Nazi regime of Germany, the Third Reich, had perfected the doctrine of racial superiority from the experiences in Namibia, Cameroon, and Tanganyika, places in Africa that had come under German control after the Berlin Conference on Africa in 1884–1885. When Adolf Hitler came to power in the 1930s, he implemented as much of the racial doctrine as he could to suppress Jews, Roma, and Africans. Three specific laws were used to express his racial doctrine:

1. *Flag law of the Reich:* When the ship *Bremen* docked in New York City in 1935, it had swastika flags, which were seen as strong symbols of anti-Semitism by many local people. A cluster of New Yorkers went to the ship, removed the swastikas, and threw them into the Hudson River. Cordell Hull, the American secretary of state, rendered an apology to the Germans.
2. *Race and citizenship law:* This law declared that Reich citizens were only those with German blood. The Nazis created a two-tier system to disempower Jews, take their businesses, and force them to leave.
3. *German blood and honor:* With this law, the Nazis claimed that only those with pure German blood could raise the German flag. There could be no race mixing, and Jewish men could not employ a German woman less than 45 years old in any job.

The First Nations people of the Americas, like those of Asia, Australia, and Africa, found themselves under threat of decimation by a white ideology bent on world conquest. In the Caribbean, where the explorer Columbus first met indigenous people on that fateful day, October 12, 1492, on the Bahamas island of San Salvador, he found a land and a people unknown to Europe who would soon be in the crucible of death and destruction. Succeeding Europeans came to the area, and the vile exploitation and enslavement of the First Nations people was one of the

Europeans' original crimes against humanity. Soon, Bartolomé de Las Casas, a priest in the Caribbean, could not take the persecution, enslavement, and brutality measured out to the native peoples, so he went to Spain in 1515 to petition the king to stop the Europeans from abusing the local people. His little book *A Short Account of the Destruction of the Indies* (1552/1992) had a powerful impact on the thinking of Europeans. Actually, they were encouraged by Las Casas to look at the Africans as a physically stronger people. In many ways, Las Casas can be called the first popular promoter of African enslavement because he articulated arguments that became standard for the defense of enslavement. Until the 16th century, European churches were regularly found to have images of black Madonnas, after the African Isis and Horus (Auset and Heru), conflated with Mary and Jesus. However, the exploration, enslavement, and colonial domination were meant to erase the memory of a common humanity. Rich Europeans commissioned artists to paint the Christian Jesus and Mother Mary as Scandinavian whites. Enslaved Africans also solidified the false image of white as superior whenever their religious inclinations turned to the "white man's religion," and therefore, like people with espadrilles walking in puddles of water, it was impossible for those Africans not to get soaked by the race paradigm. It was an effective control mechanism on a population seeking desperately to overcome a created meme used as a justification for its exploitation. Indeed, the education systems were organized as if race did not exist, but this is itself a perfect example of racism because it asserts the universality of "white" culture. Institutions tend to serve the people who established them, and so it is with school systems in the West. How do we defeat the racist expectation that blackness should be prevented from existing? For whites to accuse blacks of crimes they did not commit is an anticipated trope in the land of racism. Tamir Rice, a 12-year-old black boy, can be gunned down by police in a Cleveland, Ohio, city park, because he had a toy gun. A white man kills his white wife and then tells the police he saw a black man running away from the house.

A white mother drowns her sons and then says that two black men did it. These examples and hundreds more represent the sickening perceptual disorder caused by the racial ladder and its ascriptions.

OUR COMMON HUMANITY

On the virgin plains near the Omo River and at the river's edge in Ancient Africa, *Homo sapiens* stood up and walked. Humans prospered and lived, multiplied, and traveled to other parts of the land, and during that time, there were no multiple races that continued until now, and although there appeared, in time, many families, these did not constitute separate races. There was but one people, humans.

The advent of various ideologies of conquest, beginning with the sons' conquest of their mothers, and the dawn of patriarchy led to the hierarchical notions of one gender over others and one people over others (Kenyatta, 1962). As we have shown, the seeds were sown in the Indo-Aryan construction of castes; the Talmudic notion of different attributes for Noah's sons, Shem, Ham, and Japhet; the Arab notion of *abd* ("slave") for black people; and the European classification of "races" attached to certain characteristics in a hierarchical chain. There is little wonder that we are in the current quandary over the conception of humanity or the question of equity, equality, and justice. If we take all the concepts created since the 14th century, from ether to race, we will never discover an entity abstract and null enough to have had as much baggage around it as the false notion of race. It is, in effect, the organizer of Western civilization's most potent weapon against humanity and has become the penal colony of all failed ideas. Like ether, which was considered a rarefied elastic element accepted as permeating all spaces, including that between particles of matter, with vibrations that made light and various radiations until it was proven false, so too race as a discriminating and dangerous idea has been proven false. Of course, as far as we know, this ascripto-biological notion of hierarchy appears in just a few cultures; it is not something that was at the very beginning of human history. Western "man," perhaps the leading promoter of dualities, made it possible for ascripto-biological domination to take place in the minds of intellectuals who saw only the pure and the impure (Wynter, 2003). As we have shown, the evidence points to the European proselytizing of this concept of race in every conceivable manner. One might consider Eduardo Galeano's (1997) *Open Veins of Latin America: Five Centuries of the Pillage of a Continent* as a portrait of the stampede of Eurocentric domination of the native cultures of South America. Racial invasions and persecutions of the First Nations peoples can be seen as the superspreaders of the race virus. In southern Argentina, as in Chile and other areas of South America, the European conquest meant ruthless murders of First Nations people as if they were nonhuman, as seen in the archival information at the Museo Yamana in Ushuaia, Tierra del Fuego. Galeano's recording of the 5 centuries of plunder in Latin America can be replicated throughout that continent, as well as in Africa, Australia, and North America.

THE VIOLENCE OF HUMAN SEPARATION

Clearly, the martial and mental operations against people who were not considered white have indicated strong racial elements. This was not the ancient African way of relationships because no philosophy argued for the separation of people into human and subhuman, being and nonbeing, Jew and Gentile, Arab and heathen, or "pure" white and nonwhite. These bifurcations, honoring separateness and the attendant traits applied to various peoples, truly meant that we would have an unnecessary layer between groups of humans. These separations were not the results of strategies dictated by Africans or planned by Africans to keep apart from whites; these were the machinations of power held by whites to arrange a false reality. This schizoid order of conceptual arrangements would ultimately bring masochistic misogyny, racial bigotry, and brutal extermination of fellow humans. A society is hurried along to these results whether in anti-Dalit India, Nazi Germany, apartheid South Africa, or the segregationist United States.

What was introduced into the world by these false constructions was a poison that would rot the insides of any society and produce the most rampant forms of prejudice, discrimination, and oppression the world had ever seen. Indeed, Donald Yacovone (2020) is correct to say that white racial domination, that is, white supremacy, is a toxin that has been injected into the minds of many generations of Americans. Thus, America, and the West, have been inundated with the coarsest strand of bigotry based on the cultural construct of race. That is not to say that this toxin has not infected other people and lands, but the American and European nations, especially the United Kingdom, the United States, Germany, Portugal, and France, in their attempt to remake the world in their images have destroyed the best hope for humanity as humanity. The way forward will necessarily depend on us overcoming or at least battering down the barrier to human acceptance created by the illusion of separate races. We are one race with endless variations of physical characteristics, but our essential genetic makeup is the same. It is race that has distorted all aspects of contemporary Western society and twisted even other societies because of similar religious ideologies. Michel Foucault (1990) once said, "Power is not an institution, and not a structure; neither is it a certain strength we are endowed with; it is the name that one attributes to a complex strategical situation in a particular society" (p. 93). Having the speaking voice and the writing hand, the West described the concept of race in terms that would privilege whiteness and condemn blackness. This is the power of life over death. It is ultimately the bringer of the violence of separateness, apartheid, the separation of humans into various sectionalities.

What we have learned in our critical research is that American historians have largely ignored the embarrassing issues of America's racial history in its political, social, and economic dimensions. It is easier to speak in abstract terms about race relationships than it is to speak about the origin and promotion of racial hierarchy. This invisibility has resulted in the lack of knowledge about anything other than whiteness and Europe. We have not been surprised by our students, black and white, who often express amazement at what we consider to be some of the most obvious issues of race and racism. In some cities such as Memphis and Atlanta, there are still high school students who know nothing about the outbreaks of racist riots that drove black people out of their homes in those cities during the 19th and 20th centuries. Some students even doubt the occurrence of lynching, although in recent years there have been many books dealing with that issue. What we see among our students is a strong tendency to accept the narrative of the Tulsa riots against Black Wall Street, mainly because it has been sustained in the news via documentaries and other media. Yet the records of outbursts of violent racial acts against African Americans are shattered only by the record of abuse handed to the First Nations of Australia and the First Nations peoples of the Americas, South and North, and the Caribbean and South Pacific. Intolerance based on perceived racial superiority and racial inferiority has been allowed to flourish in too many societies in the world.

It is not necessary to present a long litany of the white supremacist attacks on Africans in America, but we believe our readers should be introduced to a few situations that have been hidden in the mainstream histories. For example, the Elaine, Arkansas, massacre of African Americans in 1919 was a vicious assault on black citizens. When black people were attacked on September 30, 1919, in Elaine, the ensuing melee became one of the bloodiest assaults on African Americans in history, where between 285 and 800 African Americans were killed. Five whites also died. Nearly 100 African American sharecroppers, those who worked on land owned by whites for a 50% share of the crops, met at church in Hoop Spur, about three miles from Elaine, with the idea of organizing a union led by the Progressive Farmers and Household Union of America. Black farmers wanted to get higher pay for their labor and for their cotton crops, which were deliberately held below the price white farmers got for their cotton crops. Under the guise of white supremacy, whites had sought to justify the unequal treatment of African farmers. A spate of racial violence against black people had occurred earlier in Washington, D.C.; Indianapolis, Indiana; Chicago, Illinois; and Knoxville, Tennessee. Racism against African American soldiers was escalating in the country because of the more confident assertion of black people speaking up for their rights at the end of the war to make the world "safe for democracy," which caused whites to feel threatened in the comfort of their ideology of white supremacy. Black soldiers who had fought overseas did not feel submissive to white people and resented the discrimination they saw when they returned to the southern states. The feeling in Elaine was the experience of black soldiers and their friends and families in other parts of the nation. This new spark of independence and freedom did not sit well with the white community, whose adoption of the illusion of race meant that they considered black people breaking through the descriptive barriers they had built in their heads a threat. Consequently, whites attacked the black freedom thinkers.

The African American guards surrounding the church where the black farmers and union leaders were meeting tried to keep the white vigilantes away from the building. A shootout occurred as the whites sought to disrupt the meeting and the black guards returned fire.

The white vigilantes retreated, but by the next morning they had reorganized and sent the sheriffs to arrest the blacks who had participated in the shootout. The posse met little or no resistance from the black community around Elaine but amassed an estimated 1,000 armed white people to "protect" what was seen as a threat to white supremacy. Ultimately, the only reason the Elaine massacre was called an insurrection was because whites felt threatened by black political organization. Yet the governor of Arkansas got federal permission to order 500 troops from the closest military base, Camp Pike, to Elaine.

On the morning of October 2, 1919, when the federal troops arrived, the white mobs and vigilante groups began to leave. The soldiers rounded up hundreds of African Americans and placed them in makeshift stockades to question them and find out if any white employer would vouch for them. The charismatic orator Robert Lee Hill, the main union organizer, was hidden by friends and later escaped to Kansas. Hill's brilliance as an organizer wrote his name in the annals of African American history in Arkansas.

Violence against African Americans seemed endemic in the United States, and in 1919, the slaughter of blacks was carried out by military soldiers and ordinary white people, who hunted African Americans and shot them down like hogs in the streets. Grif Stockley, Brian K. Mitchell, and Guy Lancaster give vivid, detailed accounts of these murders (see Stockley et al., 2020, *Blood in Their Eyes: The Elaine Massacre of 1919*). Federal troops were often called against black people in the interest of white supremacy. An employee of the newspaper *Arkansas Gazette*, named Sharpe Dunaway (1925), reported that soldiers in Elaine, Arkansas, "committed one murder after another with all the calm deliberation in the world, either too heartless to realize the enormity of their crimes, or too drunk on moonshine to give a continental darn" (p. 45; see also Stockley et al., 2020).

The Narratives of Death

The fact that American history often buries the narratives of death measured out to black people seeking equity, equality, and justice means that it is necessary to provide an Afrocentric perspective to the critical interrogations of facts in order to advance a more equitable society. We cannot simply stop at the description of the problem of race or the doctrine of white supremacy, or the consequences of these false concepts. We must begin the process of dismantling the culture that elevated the racial ascriptions to law and common practice because the idea of race as developed in this society is at the core of our problem. Harrison and D'Angelo (2021) stated quite clearly that "although science has established that there is only one biological race and humans are genetically virtually 100 percent the same, America nonetheless created a story that attributed significance for skin color" (p. 26).

While Harrison and D'Angelo are correct in their analysis of the question of race, we believe that one must add to the idea of skin color two elements, ranking and culture. This is implied in what they have written; however, at the heart of the racial anger that affects so many whites are the facts that demographics are changing and the political landscape, and hence cultural landscape, will also change, and racism will not be accepted as normal, ordinary, and proper. Therefore, the ranking of humans by racial categories, an illusionary idea that carries with it economic, social, and judicial power, is threatened and leaves racist individuals with no lodestar. Without racial superiority and without the racial ladder, they are afraid that they may become just human!

The Proud Boys and their allies who invaded the U.S. Capitol on January 6, 2021, were like a hate mob, a racist cabal, on the edge of a wild imagination, fueled by the rhetoric of Donald Trump, with the intention of taking down what they saw as a frightful, multicultural vision coming into being because of the presidential defeat of Trump. Whether they believed that the election was stolen or not, and clearly it was not stolen, they exhibited the same fierce determination to grab humanity by the neck and choke possibility to death. It was likened to a lynch mob, orchestrated by the sitting president of the United States, who sought a coup against the winning candidate for the presidency, Joe Biden.

Democracies often spur insurrections. When a mass of people do not like the fact that their candidate or candidates did not win an election, they can choose to wait for another election or they can criminally create an insurrection. Both examples are found in the American nation. Although history is replete with angry outbreaks of violence around issues of racial equality, few have been successful in turning back the pages of humanity.

Since President Andrew Johnson pardoned those individuals who had fought to retain the enslavement of Africans, the United States has been dealing with the remnants of a racist stain on the society. The Civil War could have been a revolution that would have overthrown the symbols, icons, and images of a warped system of racial categories. However, the fact that so many members of the society sympathized with the loss of absolute domination that the white southerners felt with the abolishment of the enslavement meant that the American government would be strapped for generations with the insidious race doctrine that led to ideas of white supremacy.

Almost immediately after the end of the Civil War, the city of New Orleans, where whites and blacks were in close contact, descended into the ugly mob characteristics that would come to define the southern response to race. The New Orleans Massacre of 1866 happened a little over a year and two months after the surrender of General Lee to General Grant at Appomattox, Virginia. A group of African Americans demonstrated for their rights under freedom and were immediately set on by white mobs from throughout the city. It appeared that among the ranks of the rioters who attacked the black demonstration were former soldiers of the defeated Confederacy. More than 40 African Americans were killed during the white riot of July 1866.

Less than 10 years later, on September 14, 1874, the Crescent City White League attempted an insurrection against the elected Republican integrated slate of officers in what was termed the Battle of Canal Street. Nearly 5,000 whites in paramilitary gear marched with Confederate symbols to the police station and fought with the state militia and police as they attacked the statehouse, all government buildings, and the armory. For three days, the insurgents held all the buildings in downtown New Orleans, which was the capital of Louisiana at the time, while demanding that their slate of candidates be seated. The federal troops had to enter the city and put down the insurrection; however, not one insurgent was charged with a crime, although more than 20 people were reported murdered.

Yet the 1898 Wilmington, North Carolina, insurrection, often called a massacre or coup, which erupted against an elected body of black and white officials, was probably the most heralded insurrection by white southerners. Angry that blacks had been elected to political office, nearly 2,000 white supremacists formed the mob that attacked the black community on November 10, 1898. The mayhem caused by the insurrectionists caused black and white politicians of the Fusionist Party to leave the city, whereon, the mob destroyed city property, firebombed the businesses of the black citizens who had voted, and destroyed the only black newspaper in the city. It is estimated that the crazed rioters killed up to 300 people. This action led to the direct removal and replacement of elected officials by a mob.

The Human Condition

The frosty pane through which racists see themselves often distorts their images of themselves. They are not saviors; they are illusionists who have swallowed the pill of delusion caused by the idea of race. This is precisely why we say that racism is a system of categories organized by white people to enforce hierarchical relationships based on phenotypes. Nothing has agitated the racists more than the political election of black or white people who have abandoned the race categories, because racists believe that politics is the expression of power and they cannot see themselves associating with Africans, Asians, or Native People on an equal basis. The "master race" ideology dictates that they must reduce other people to inferior positions. Of course, fascism, as in Nazi Germany, becomes one of the expressions of that desire to elevate one's own so-called race to the top of the ladder while suppressing any other people. In effect, this becomes an ideological regime that centralizes autocratic and dictatorial power in the hands of one person or group who organizes society around rules and regimentations meant to stamp out freedom. Those who are antifascists are merely against all autocracies of race, class, or gender.

During the 21st century, we must begin the dismantling of the false planks of race to rebuild the most ancient idea of humanity as one race. Clearly in the United States, people have tended to associate white supremacy with the practice of enslavement and overt attacks on black people. There is some truth in this idea, but it should be understood that the doctrine of white supremacy is not merely an attribute of the southerner in American history. As an ideology, the doctrine of white supremacy is a part of the imperial, colonial, technocratic, neoliberal Pan-European Academy and an entire basket of antihuman, semireligious mythologies whereby Europeans from the 15th to the 20th century sought to impose their wills and egos through their militaries, merchants, and missionaries on the rest of the world in the grand scheme of honoring Greek and Roman heroes as the models of white dominance. So deeply implanted into the hearts of whites was the idea of their superiority that even those whites during the Enslavement Period who were against slavery often felt that whites were significantly "different" from Africans. In effect, whites could be against slavery and yet see black people as aliens, not quite human. Africans were said to have extravasate blood, capable of infecting the entire body of white people. Even today, there are probably whites who believe that blacks are of a different order than themselves, even though they would proclaim loudly that they promote equality of opportunity!

The work of two Russian anthropologists and Africanists has challenged our common understanding of hierarchy with a novel theory. Dmitri Bondarenko and Andrey Korotayev have proposed the concepts of heterarchy and homoarchy (Bondarenko, 2006; Bondarenko & Korotayev, 2000). For them, *heterarchy* is the relation of elements to one another when they are unranked or when they possess the potential for being ranked in a number of different ways. This, they claim, is not the opposite of hierarchy altogether but finds its explanatory value as the opposite of *homoarchy*, which can be defined as the relation of elements to one another when they are rigidly ranked one way only and thus possess very little potential for being unranked or ranked in another or a number of different ways, at least without cardinal reshaping of the whole sociopolitical order. To put it clearly, *heterarchy* exists when people live among each other without the ascripto-biological hierarchy one finds in racist societies. This unranked existence, however, is not the opposite of hierarchy but rather the opposite of *homoarchy*, which occurs when we live with one another in rigidly ranked societies with only one possibility. One normally thinks of caste systems, as in India, in this sense. However, *homoarchy* was fundamentally the system of American enslavement and white South African apartheid for many years. The irrational idea was to separate humans from humans as part of maintaining a ranking system.

It is important to remember that Americans are trained to see racism as a result of southern slavery, exhibited by actors with visible images of the Ku Klux Klan, promoted by rabid demagogues shouting racial epithets. First of all, slavery was in the North as well as in the South, and the people who formed the idea of American identity were not southern slave owners but northerners, such as the 19th century propagandist John H. Van Evrie, born in 1814, probably in Canada. Evrie practiced medicine, but his main profession was white racial propaganda. In fact, he popularized the idea of white supremacy as part of his American identity. He was the editor of the *Weekly Day Book* and the author of several pamphlets on race and slavery written for the ordinary white audience. When he founded the publishing company Van Evrie, Horton & Company, he used it as a tool for spreading his white supremacist ideas. Although racists have existed before Van Evrie, he is literally the first person who made a profession of attacking blacks and elevating whites, along with propagating what he called the natural order (Horsman, 1981). There was no significant scientific evidence ever presented by Van Evrie, yet he promoted and defended African enslavement, attacked abolitionists, asserted white superiority, and found no reason for what he called class distinctions between white people. Indeed, Van Evrie thought that enslavement was a good thing because otherwise European class distinctions would have followed whites to America and created conflict. In effect, white supremacy was necessary to give ordinary working-class whites a buffer between them and the propertied class. Van Evrie published a pamphlet previously called *Negroes and Negro "Slavery"* under the neologism *Subgenation: The Theory of the Normal Relation of the Races* and subtitled *An Answer to "Miscegenation."* The title referred to what Van Evrie called the natural relationship of an inferior to a superior race. For him, racial domination was the centerpiece of American democracy and the vital principle of American society (see Kaplan, 1991).

It should be clear that Van Evrie was not alone in propaganda; it is just that he made it his principal duty, becoming what might be called today a professional propagandist for racism. Now that so many other publicists, politicians, preachers, and authors have made white supremacy a standard for all political discourses around race, we must seriously think about how to bring down this house of race. This preoccupation with race conceals the desire for dominance and control. No wonder the old white man standing in the doorway of a faded white country store in Arkansas asked the young African American man who had stopped for gasoline on his trip from Texas to Tennessee, "Nigger, are you a Negro?" Stunned, the young man said, "Sir, I am an African." To which the old white man replied, "You look like a Negro to me."

The reason this becomes important is because without dismantling the racial ladder we will never be able to get to the point that Kendi (2019) demands—changing the policies of the nation. The policies are derived from a culture steeped in the doctrine of white supremacy, and our collective task as concerned citizens and abused people of Africa has been to combat the racial ideas promoted by this doctrine. The negating policies are derived from the belief in the racial ladder; it must be removed from our thinking to make for a more perfect human unity. It is not enough to declare the ladder is false or to say it is dead; we must in fact take it down step by step until the ladder is itself gone.

How to Become Humans Being Human

Our practical objective is to dismantle the *House of Race* to erect the *House of Humanity*. To dismantle means to take a structure apart piece by piece and, if necessary, throw the pieces into the trash heap of history. This requires us to revisit the structure, examine its central parts, and remove them from the angle of our perspective in order to provide an avenue toward recuperating the society. We know that the common wisdom is that this cannot be done because the structure has been here for centuries, but all ideas and ideologies can be transformed, found useless, dispensed with, and replaced with other and perhaps better ideas and ideologies.

The human project is grounded in the optimistic belief that human beings are capable of seeing truth and then transforming themselves and their societies. Of course, this involves taking the concept of whiteness out of the default position in discourses about people in America. Whiteness as a concept will have to take its place alongside, not above, other categories. It is to be seen neither through some negation of other people nor as being the opposite of cultures considered inferior barbaric, degraded or effeminate. There are occasions when the so-called white category is stratified to the position where some whites are seen as inferior to other whites. Hence, the Italian, Spaniard, Greek, and Albanian is not like the German, English, or Dutch. The perception of these Mediterranean types was that they were too close to Africa and therefore backward. One could argue that this is not true; however, it was a perception that did not wear off among the white supremacists. America's dynamic ethno-racial configuration had come to be seen as African Americans, Asian Americans, whites, Native Americans, and Latinx. Clearly, the American situation would demand an analysis that considered the perceptions of the ethnic pentad as well as the Mediterranean whites as part of the resistance to white supremacy. Various theories such as Afrocentricity, decoloniality, and deconstruction have been employed to understand the complexities of the vestiges of power and domination. Like the embers of a dying fire, the vestiges of white supremacy, as seen in the attempted seizure of the Capitol building on January 6, 2021, can still cause a burning fire. In the end, however, the darkness will come, and one of humanity's most enduring penal colonies, race, will be banished from the earth.

When one looks at the decolonial movement, especially in South America and Africa, one is tempted to think of similar situations in North America; however, this could only be true if we were to consider white Americans as victims of colonialism. There are, in fact, those whites who found their integration into the world of Europe without giving up their American political inheritance a win-win for white supremacy. When one speaks of coloniality and decoloniality in the contemporary sense, one must be clear that this is speech about European coloniality in Africa or South America, not in North America. The American nation, in its white-controlled capacity, would not ever be perceived as a colonialism situation in the same fashion as Africans or South Americans. In America, it was African Americans who were discriminated against, denied an episteme, racially punished for being black, and dispossessed materially. There is no innocence in the lives of black people; there is only resistance, defiance, and struggle to achieve freedom. Black people have taken this position because the end of anti-African policies, like all racist policies, is the pursuit of the ultimate extermination of the target people. We have seen this throughout history in reference to the Native peoples of the Americas and Australia, the Jewish people of Germany and Poland, and the Africans in Namibia, Congo, and many other places. Even so, humans, African humans, have no intention of allowing this age to be a time of unprotected victims. We Africans decided over the decades that it was impossible to participate in the condemnation of blackness. Living through the dystopian era of anti-Africanism, one gets the sense that we are experiencing Octavia Butler's *Parable of the Sower* (1993) or George Orwell's *1984* (1949) or Albert Camus's *The Plague* (1948).

What are the characteristics that underpin white supremacy in the American society, and by extension the world society? Here is the reality of the situation. A society created by people who believe in their superiority is delusional. To support their delusion, they must deny others any form of humanity. In fact, they suggest that there is no autonomy, no freedom, and no identity for African people, except as subhuman. Harrison and D'Angelo (2021) state this quite directly:

> The fabrication of a new type of categorization of humanity was needed because the leaders of the American colonies at the turn of the 18th century had deliberately selected Africans to be permanent slaves. In the era when the dominant political philosophy was equality, civil rights, democracy, justice and freedom for all human beings, the only way Christians could justify slavery was to demote Africans to nonhuman status. (p. 27)

Since white supremacists see themselves as the only humans, they are prepared to mutilate, brutalize, and kill all others who seek to express their autonomy. The so-called superior race takes the position that it has the will and the right to dominate other people as a matter of nature. It is like Hitler's Third Reich army decrying their loss at Stalingrad and bemoaning the fact that Aryans had been defeated by Slavs!

The language of the white supremacist is dyadic: ethical and unethical, beautiful and ugly, consent and dissent, power and weakness; but always the white supremacist sees herself or himself in the superior position. This is why we have claimed in the search for humanity that we cannot disconnect ourselves from our African origin, our common ancestry, and our visible and invisible networks created in the generational linkages that stretch back thousands of years. Afrocentrists claim that our ancient history, that is, the ancient Kemetic and Nile Valley legacies, are in direct conflict with human unequal dyads, racialized distinctions of humans, and dichotomies created to separate children of the same family of *Homo sapiens sapiens*. Even the ancient temple, shrines, and sacred sites reflected the idea of harmony. Actually, Herodotus tells us that the most celebrated oracles of the ancient world were located in Kemet: the oracle of Hercules at Canopis, Apollo at Apollinopolis Magna, Minerva at Sais, Diana at Bubastis, Mars at Papremis, and Jupiter at Thebes and Ammonium. Furthermore, we know, according to Herodotus (2013, *Histories*, 2.42–2.57), that the Greek oracles were Egyptian imitations. But the ancient oracles did not distinguish between peoples or assume a racial ladder. It is for this reason that we must reexamine the pre-nightmare experiences of African people to assert a new dimension of the human.

Afrocentrists insist that difference does not have to bring acrimony, just because we do not speak the same language or have the same complexions or gender as other humans. Once again, we emphasize the trans-ethnic nature of Ma'at, translated as truth, justice, righteousness, harmony, order, balance, and reciprocity. In southern and eastern Africa, the idea of *Ubuntu* or *Chivanhu* in the regions where people speak Nguni, Xhosa, and Shona is an extension of the ancient Maatic ideal—thus, values such as respect, accountability, discipline, unity, dignity, self-determination, cooperation, and respect for humanity. This is why Artwell Nhemachena and colleagues (2020) define humanity in terms of *huntu/unhu* and not simply in terms of vitality/agency.

As we have demonstrated in the earlier chapters, the assault on African people has been persistent in the Western world since the presence of imperial colonialism. White supremacy operates the racial ladder to its advantage by representing Africans and First Nations people as those without civilization and therefore at the bottom of the ladder. Of course, the position is arrogant and delusional, but it sits at the bedside of the most inane, racist ideologies. No people are without history, without technological innovations, or without discovery and traditions. This is why we agree with Nhemachena et al. (2020) when they write,

> African humanism is traceable not necessarily to the European Enlightenment but to precolonial African Chivanhu/Ubuntu. Put differently, the Enlightenment humanised Europeans some of whom became colonialists who dehumanised African people whom they subjected to [data] colonialism.... Because *hunhu/unhu*, which should also be applied in research, existed even during the precolonial era, scholars in Africa note that African humanity/humanism and human rights did not necessarily emanate from the European Enlightenment. (p. 108)

Like their ancient ancestors of the Nile Valley, the people of *Ubuntu* and *hunhu* understood that humans were complete with the gift of Ma'at. There was no evolution; when a child was born into a family, he or she came into existence as a human with all of the powers of humanity. The introduction of white racial supremacy as an ideology, and all other hierarchies of class or caste before the colonialism of the Europeans, meant the pollution of the perfect understanding that was bestowed on us by our first ancestors, who knew that to be human meant the obliteration of all meaningful distinctions and the elevation of people to Maatic beings capable of a universal and common relationship. Because of this reality, it is necessary for us to destroy the structures supporting the false notion of white supremacy. All doctrines of racial or national superiority based on physical characteristics must be abandoned to the trash heaps of irrationality.

Think of white racial supremacy as a building with all of the elements necessary to establish its presence. It will have a foundation. It will have several rooms with several capabilities. It will have a roof. It will have walls. And it will have occupants who use the various rooms for special activities.

How do you go about dismantling that structure, particularly if it is supported by a cadre of defenders of the illusion who will do anything to keep it from being dismantled? We know that the doctrine of white supremacy is one of the most dominant blocks in the wall of race because it has lasted for centuries. Thus, when we speak of de-superiorization or decolonization, we are most likely referring to the necessary activity of demobilizing the action that produces the false ideologies. Although it is only since the 20th century, the era of assembling the tools for dismantling, that a serious assault has been mounted against white supremacy by those who support a common humanity, we have not forgotten that white identity is the basic expression of what is often called the American identity or that when people talk of Western civilization, they frequently mean *white* civilization. An American citizen can be a person from a variety of cultural or national origins, and none of them must be white.

Here is what we know about the way the West has structured reality. There is a house of race built on a sandy foundation and a house of humanity built on a rocky foundation. One is well fortified with the asymmetry of authority that comes from control of information dissemination by whites vis-à-vis Africans, Asians, and Latinx in the United States. The levers of power are stuck in a hegemonic position. The other house, as we shall see, starts from a different foundation, one established when our ancestors figured out how to solve the problem of human continuity, something that had to be done to ensure the survival of every human. Consider what our research and experiences have taught us about the enduring characteristics of the old and descending house of race, and then, examine what we know about the revivified and ascending house of humanity.

House of Race
Patriarchy
White supremacy
Hierarchy of "races"
Hierarchy of gender
Highlighting alterity
Weaponizing physical traits
Assertion of Anglo-Germanic or Aryan superiority
Belief that race is approved by nature and deities
Toxic relationships with all other people
Self-centered greed
Exploitation of non-white people
Deceitful interactions

House of Humanity
Homo sapiens
Commonalities outweigh differences
Acceptance of difference
Respect for life
Dignity in being human
Humility facing difference
Cooperation over competition

African culture, as Fifteenth Ferreira understood and portrayed it in her book *The Demise of the Inhuman: Afrocentricity, Modernism, and Postmodernism* (2015), might be our best hope of holding back chaos because it is founded on the principle of harmony and not conflict, the idea of unity of beings and not divisions, and the idea that spirituality is the making sacred of the earth and the relationships in it. One could say that everything is spiritual so long as we know that to be spiritual means to be in perfect relationship with ourselves and others; beyond this is nothing but mystery as deep as the runic signals in some archaic alphabet long forgotten by contemporary humans. Economics is nothing but relationship, so is curriculum, as is war and peace. We are nothing as humans if we do not have or do not engage in the constant process of making humanity. All forms of activities, whether digital or natural, in this century or in centuries long gone are interconnected and can be seen, in a narrow way, as intersectional, not con-sectional, as in conflict.

To complete the process of dismantling the house of race and erecting the house of humanity, we must re-envision humanity as one people with relatively insignificant variations of phenotypes. This calls for action on every communication and educational front where we will be able to effectively transform assessments of history, sociology, and other social sciences while at the same time introducing a new episteme and cultural meme deriving from the most ancient value of Ma'at. Textbooks, digital and physical, will have to be modified; curricula in all schools and colleges will have to be rewritten to reflect the unity of humanity; and there will have to be radical changes in the political culture of the West and the East—especially in India, for example, with its long history of persecuting the Dalits; in Australia, with its disrespect and disregard for the Aboriginal First Nations, and in the Americas, where the First Nations have been denied their own lands and cultures because of the imposition of Europe.

Now we are fundamentally aware that there are some important cultural implications that need to be considered in terms of our search for the house of humanity. Based on all the evidence that we have, stemming from the disciplines of biology, archaeology, anthropology, genetics, astronomy, geology, botany, and so on, we know that Africa is the home of humanity and the original *Homo sapiens* human culture that left Africa was African matriarchy, based on the reciprocity and harmony between the woman and the man. Logically, it was in the interest of women and men to forge an alliance in order to produce life and culture. We have tried to show that patriarchal domination was a newer culture, developed in more difficult, harsher climes where life was less bountiful. We are saying that the aggressive control of women by men, reflected in all institutions, family, health, economics, politics, spirituality, entertainment, and education, affects the development or underdevelopment of the societies in which it is manifested. Moreover, based on the fundamental values, beliefs, theories, and behaviors that have ensued from these two cultural forms, we have argued that patriarchal power relations provided the basis for the cultural construction of race. In this way, we have conceptually tied the behaviors and beliefs in injustice, the first being that of domination by man over woman, to the invention of the hierarchy of humanity. It will be necessary to understand that both of these cultures, which stand in direct opposition to each other, were believed in and practiced as cultural norms. As Africologists, we have sought to interrogate Africa for the solution to our situation of facing the construction of race, whereby we are the victims, in that our lives appear worth less than other lives on the ladder of race and black/African women, men, and children across the world have our lands and lives stolen every day.

There is every reason to suggest that African matriarchy, the reciprocity between women and men, is the authentic foundation of democracy, justice, truth, harmony, balance, honesty, peace, and compassion. These are the principles critical to real progress in our search for humanity. These are the lived principles that grew out of a harmonious relationship between women and men. When we consider the myriad negative portrayals that African and/or black humanity have borne and suffered endlessly as the opposite of who we are, through religion, politics, academia, education, and the media, it begs credulity that we are still here in spite of the construction of a distorted belief in evolution, progress, and advancement whereby we are still considered, in the deep psyche of the European and some South Asian patriarchies, sinners who would forever pay the price; "beasts" closer to the ape than the human, and the devil, evil in character and ugly in looks, black in countenance and carriage. All these racist concepts are theoretically grounded inside patriarchy.

The focus on evolution, progress, and the future suggests that African/black humanity would disappear as the weakest beast in the struggle for existence while the beautiful, wise, knowledgeable, intelligent, well-mannered, gracious, kind, academically gifted, sweet-smelling, genteel, generous, kind, articulate, and so on, so-called white men, women, and children, with least melanin, will survive as we move through time to a better world. We, African people, having our cultural memory in Africa know these ancient values of democracy, justice, truth, reciprocity, harmony, balance, love, compassion, and honesty, and that is why over all the centuries of disdain, we have fought for liberation and freedom against these hostile cultures that have claimed these lofty ideals but never fulfilled them. Countless millions of us have fought and died to change these vile, unprincipled ways of living.

So how do evolution and progress on the way to civilization from barbarism apply to women, men, and children of the darkest hue? It cannot. Staying within the Africological concepts, we examine Maatian principles and values, the earliest ethical system, as the quintessential definition of civilization. These ideas came from those of the darkest hue, considered today by many Europeans to be descended from beasts, whose enslavement and continuing discrimination are considered punishment for being black and the descendants of a man, not black, who cursed his son for castrating him by condemning all black people to be enslaved forever. Of course, the real history and herstory reveal what Count Volney recognized in the 1700s when visiting Egypt, that Africa's Kemet, home to the blackest women, men, and children, taught the world civilization and the highest levels of science, mathematics, and spirituality, and gave us principles by which to live, writings that taught ways to become human and how to make and use medicines and healings that would help us survive, agriculture that was shared, nonhierarchical ways to harmonize and exist with nature, and welcoming ways of treating each other. This is antithetical to evolutionist theory, as Diop understood when he wrote *Civilization or Barbarism: An Authentic Anthropology*, published in English in 1992. We have two choices. We can go toward barbarism, or we can go toward humanity. Our objective is to culturally inform readers about the role of Africa in human civilization because without this knowledge we remain ignorant and undeterred by the imposition of a false reality. The dominators have been very resolute in making sure that those who speak of a civilizing and humanizing Africa are maligned and debased and those who follow the Pan-European/Arabo academic route are rewarded and considered "real" and "serious" academics. Those black academics who buy into the belief in Africa's barbarism are sadly placing their own integrity in the hands of their academic, Euro-Arabo scholastic fathers, who are often anti-black and anti-African. Our position is clear: Do not fear to look back, for we must learn who we are and take the best from what we have been to build a future where humanity can prosper. We are asking that those who believe in race look outside the paradigm to see reality and future possibilities in the context of *sankofa*, returning to fetch what was left behind, in order to educate ourselves and develop cultural identities forged into humanity. So far, for Europeans and Southwest Asian people (Arabic, Iranians, Indian, etc.) to follow the teachings of African people that have been plagiarized and lost their earlier forms as a result of cultures antithetical to those of the darkest hue in all countries is not allowed as evolution tells us falsely that black people are savages below the facade. Indeed, it is the other way around. We may look to the hundreds of millions of women, men, and children who have been wiped off the face of the earth by the perpetuators and perpetrators of barbarism as though this is a necessary behavior for the good of humanity. Understanding that our thoughts, behaviors, actions, beliefs, values, and alliances are all culturally grounded frees us up to step out of the genetic notions of race that stultify our human development, falsely categorized as genetic, and enables us to step outside this construct and prepare to place true education, the route to enlightenment, at the fore in moving forward with new ideas on how pro-human culture, the original culture that is our heritage and our legacy, can change the ongoing patriarchal racist institutions. In this role, we seek an innovative, energized population of young scholars and intellectuals led by the intensely conscious African youth who are committed to abandoning the past and embracing the future.

These are tasks for the courageous, who with ingenuity and defiance will stand at Eshu's crossroads and send us in the right direction for human success. In our judgment, the energy to transform an entire culture will demand that the imposed on, the dominated, the abused rise to the occasion of asserting their own agency. It is only then that we will be able to accept transformation as a legitimate instrument of reeducating our society. Miseducation is one of the problems, but it is not the only issue we will face when we seek to introduce humanity as the principal meme of world culture.

The new cadre of transformers will have to have a commitment to freedom; they cannot be fragile and must not accept fragility or the fear of intimidation as a reason to ignore humanity. No issues should be off limits to the transformation. Why is it that white teachers fear teaching about the enslavement of African people? Why is it that black people fear white teachers talking about the enslavement? Why is it that some white politicians have a problem with teaching any children about the actual facts of history? All barriers must be broken in the interest of humanity. The reason this issue introduces fear and fragility is because most Americans still live in the race house. If you live in the race house, you will have several ways to look at these issues. A white person living in the race house will feel that they cannot talk about enslavement without revealing their feelings about the racial ladder; that is, they believe that whites are superior, so how could they really be honest in their conversation about enslavement? They recognize that it is not socially or politically correct to be for slavery, but they do not want to be exposed in the race house. There are black people who also live in the race house constructed by white people, and they feel that a discussion of enslavement will automatically place the gaze on black people as inferior to white people. These issues have to be confronted head-on to change the equation in the society to one of a common humanity. This means that textbooks must be scrutinized and brushed clean of racist ideologies, racial ladder thinking, and untruthful and inaccurate narrative about African people. Furthermore, media outlets will have to participate in the drive for humanity and the negation of negativity about other people. The term "race" will have to be disposed of, challenged, and questioned at every possible turn in order to sweep clean the floor established as the foundation for white supremacy. We are making this bold declaration in the face of the very excellent works that have been written on race. In fact, the Fanonian notion of race inspired an entire generation with race talk. Since Frantz Fanon was a revolutionary thinker during the 1950s and 1960s and gave his era a liberation philosophy based on a rejection of racism, he became an icon in the struggle for human freedom. What Fanon believed was that the concept of blackness had to be asserted so that whites would see that the use of race as created by Western society was a part of white subjectivity. Indeed, this is why he saw the discourse around race as the central issue in Western civilization. It introduces a topic that is avoided if possible in the West or shunned to the margins of all polite discussions. Fanon knew, as many Afrocentrists and decolonial scholars know, that even if race is not mentioned explicitly, it is tucked into the conversation in most American homes in an implicit fashion. Fanon understood that the lack of recognition of black people by white people did not mean that whites, who were overrepresented as human, respected blacks. Whites have brutalized and punished black bodies for being black and have asserted ad infinitum the authority of whites to peddle their ideology of race. Many Europeans saw Fanon as preaching a kind of anti-white philosophy where violence in the possession of the downtrodden and oppressed was seen as a good value. Fanon published *Black Skin, White Masks* (1952/2008), and it immediately became one of the most popular books among African revolutionaries. It was followed by *Things Fall Apart* (1961/2001) and other writings. However, the race paradigm would be discovered by African American scholars as a boon to their own research. Kimberlé Crenshaw, a law professor at the University of California–Los Angeles, founded critical race theory and advanced the idea of intersectionality from her work in feminist legal theory, sexism, race, racism, and law. For Crenshaw, intersectionality is a lens that allows one to see where power emerges and collides and where it interlocks and intersects. In this construction, one does not see a race problem, a class problem, or a gender problem in isolation but rather as a point where one is able to acknowledge that everyone has a unique perspective on their own problems of discrimination and prejudice and that is why all aspects must be considered when examining oppression of any type. Crenshaw views gender, race, class, sexual orientation, and physical ability as points for intersectionality. What happens if there is no race? Would being human lessen the intersectionality that is hyped by race as a paradigm? We raise these questions because they are at the center of our constant battle with the persistence of racism. The pursuit of the human disrupts race and gender. It does not abolish them, but it destroys the need for discursive arguments related to rankings. We have no debate with either critical race theory or posthumanism since our position is that they are both equally unnecessary in a world where we have assumed and envisioned the human.

Therefore, to eliminate race as a point of society's concern, it is necessary to give the country, indeed the Western world, the stern medicine that it has been avoiding for many years. There can never be a model democracy without the maturity to face its past in all of its horror. To teach the truth is to provide children the basis for making logical decisions and therefore to enable them to make sense of the call for national unity. Otherwise, having drunk the milk of white supremacy and the racial ladder, the society will continue to produce nothing but wind. We want more; we need more; and therefore, we are willing to risk losing a few to the forest of racial poverty. Whatever we do for the future of the nation must be first done for the survival of African people, whose intake of toxic lethality from the society makes genocide a part of the process of American democracy. Killing black people has gone on for too long; the time is out for cowards whose identities are captured in fear-based notions of their superiority. They are neither superior, nor are they supermen or superwomen in genius or physicality. They are human just like the rest of us, and they have no advantage bequeathed to them because of their paler faces. Such an incredibly crippling delusion has created alternative realities that lead people to make bad judgments. So then, what is it to be human? How is *Maaticity* actualized in the real world?

The human sees humanity in his or her own face and that of the neighbor. To be human is to assert dignity-affirming responses to all people, plants, and animals. By doing this, one reflects the ancient principles of Ma'at as established thousands of years ago in the Nile Valley civilizations. In the West, one usually distinguishes between humans, plants, and animals; yet in the philosophy of classical Africa, humans were considered a part of the same universe as plants and animals, living things. In fact, how one treats living things and nonliving things in the environment can be seen as a determining factor in declaring one's humanity. How can a person who trashes the forests, pollutes the ocean, and poisons the atmosphere declare humanity if, as we have said, humanity is about dignity-affirming actions?

Bantu Stephen Biko said in *I Write What I Like* (2002), "In time we shall be in position to bestow upon South Africa the greatest gift possible—a more human face" (p. 2). A visionary perspective is one that moves our thinking from race to humanity; this is what Biko was able to elevate in the midst of the worst racial crisis in the world at the time of his challenge to a diabolical apartheid. All forms of racial cruelty, such as the rape of women, castration of men, enslaving of children, caging of immigrant children like animals, or beating of Dalit people for walking on sidewalks, must come to an end. Who can see what is done in the name of race, religion, or creed and not declare a moratorium and punishment for such behavior?

It is not enough that we have examined the foundations of the race illusion; we must make concrete recommendations that will advance our common humanity, such as the following:

> Stop killing black people because of race.
> Stop killing any people because of race, religion, or gender.
> Stop divesting black people of economic power.
> Stop assuming based on color or caste that black people are criminal.
> Stop disempowering people because of race, caste, gender, or religion.
> Stop protecting police, security forces, and politicians who trade in racial rhetoric.
> Stop promoting white people who preach the spurious racial superiority doctrine.
> Stop advancing organizations that discriminate on the basis of race.
> Embrace humanity.
> Embrace commonality of opportunity and possibility.
> Embrace all children as teachable.
> Embrace the beauty of diversity.
> Embrace the African origin of humanity.
> Embrace all colors and complexions of humans as equal.
> Embrace the common human quest to protect the earth's environment.
> Embrace a common quest for cultural pluralism.
> Embrace cultural differences as the human rainbow.

Each of us must be purveyors of a humanity that seeks to eliminate race in all structures and complexes of power. Working in the social sciences, we have arrived at the point where we know how the disempowerment of Africans works in the real world constructed by racists; it is a world that must be confronted in every social science and taken down piece by piece until we are able to emerge as the free humans we aspire to be.

Lee D. Baker, as pointed out earlier, wrote the famous book *From Savage to Negro: Anthropology and the Construction of Race, 1896–1954* in 1998, in which he declared anthropology to be one of the most significant racist disciplines in the Pan-European Academy. In one of his courses, Baker (2011) said,

> Racial categories are very real social and cultural phenomena. They are rooted in history and culturally constructed through laws, the media, and various institutions. These categories are reproduced, subverted, and sometimes changed by people through socialization, media consumption, interaction, dialogue, protest, and political participation. Yet, what makes race real, animates it with so much power, and fosters its tenacious hold on much of the Western world's collective psyche? It is the fact that people largely believe that race has something to do with nature, biology, or rational science. Ironically, it is biology and so-called natural sciences that provides the best evidence that there is no valid basis to organize people by racial categories. (p. 1)

Not only is Baker correct in his assumptions about anthropology, but he also suggests that at the core of the discipline is the Western world's shaping of our thoughts about race. All findings of anthropology prior to the 20th century are wrapped in the fabric of the categories of race. Therefore, it is necessary that an entirely new group of anthropologists be raised who will challenge the tired and tortured classifications of Euro-America based on morphology, pigmentation, and skulls.

The rhetoric of race as introduced in the European construction carries with it a dignity deficit for all people not included in the compact for white supremacy. Whether it is the African who encounters the European in the 15th century or the Indigenous Americans, the First Nations of the Americas and the Caribbean, who meet the whites on the sandy beaches, the idea of white superiority emerged to bring about a heinous racial disregard of other people. Alterity, even as discussed by poststructuralists and decolonialists, is itself at the heart of the race idea. This is one of the principal reasons why Africologists have declared war on all forms of alterity. One should look at this as the assertion of human agency and not as the denial of difference. Cultural differences on the basis of heritage, legacies, or experiential backgrounds are real, but they can never be shaped as denying the authenticity of people whose backgrounds are dissimilar.

We know that the ancestors of the Africans who were transported across the Atlantic Ocean to the Americas never held beliefs that distinguished the secular from the holy or, in other words, the ordinary from the sanctified. In effect, the separation of phenomena in this bifurcated way was on the arc of European thinking as whites approached Africans and Native Americans. The African concept of reality remains an interconnected system of wholeness. As humans, we are totally intertwined with nature and with one another in the united flowing of the river of being. Nothing human is separated as sacred or secular in and of itself; all things are named and respected or despised by virtue of our own human choosing. While the African has chosen the idea of unity, Europe often sees the sacred and the secular as opposite positions.

Others before us have claimed that sexuality created a hierarchy between the Roman Catholic, and perhaps Orthodox Catholic, clergy and the masses they served. The clergy were not supposed to engage in sex so that they might conserve sperm and blood, while the masses, less holy, could indeed participate in sexuality so long as it was regulated. Such thinking led to the creation of ideas of purity and impurity, the civilized and the savages, and the perfect and the blemished.

There is no intellectual duality found in the African character; there is always movement toward wholeness. Hence, we claim a need to draw back from separations, dualities, crises, and conflicts. It is in this moment that humans are presented with the decision to engage or to encounter, that is, to confront that which is different, other humans as not being human; indeed, we see that some are often called subhuman in the race model.

Aníbal Quijano's claim that the "racism/ethnicism complex" is responsible for contemporary modernity is similar to Robert Farris Thompson's (1984) idea that Africans created the modern world. European modernity is identical to Europe's moment of racial hubris, colonial passion, and aggressive imperialism (Thompson, 1984). All major crises of contemporary society can be traced to the racial ideologies of the past 500 years, and issues of gender, ethnic cleansing, sexual orientation, climate change due to global warming, and class deprivations can be tied to the practices and discourses around white supremacy. Even recent immigrants from Turkey, Mexico, Iran, Iraq, Haiti, China, Korea, and Thailand could claim "whiteness" and distance themselves from blacks, who occupy the bottom of the imaginary racial ladder. Hence, the continuation of the racial practice that supports white dominance can have a global reach.

Our insistence is for social, economic, and cultural justice. The pivot of the 21st-century Black Lives Matter movement is our reward for staying the course of resistance to colonial, racial, and class dominations. Police brutality was not merely out of hand, which had been the case since the early 20th century after the Reconstruction ended, it had become much more brazen and public. The Black Lives Matter movement caught it by the neck and held it accountable for the wanton murders of black men and women. The movement was joined by thousands of people who also saw the humanity of this action.

There were those individuals who refused to be seduced by the pleas for multiculturalism, where white people stood at the top and directed by design all others to come under their umbrella. They saw the fallacy of this position. There were those who rejected the institutional calls for Africans to self-subordinate to the hegemony of whiteness. They knew that no humans are below or above others on the basis of false ideas of racial or caste rankings. There were those who wanted to enable would-be-masters to pit black people against browns, yellows, immigrants, or poor whites, in an endless war for meager resources already parceled out by color. We were not fooled by the talk of an intellectual revolution or an end to fundamental religious doctrines, or economic humanism that still left white racial domination in charge of the reality. So-called white people had to join with the rest of the world to combat separation, not difference but the idea that you can treat one human one way and another a different way without moral or ethical sanctions. Thus, we articulate the aspirations of the Afro-Iraqi, the Dalits, the Afro-Mexicans, the Afro-Iranian, the Afro-Turks, and the infinite and diverse representatives of the human population whose hue might exist in shade. In a real sense, Aníbal Quijano is right in "*Qué tal Raza!*" when he proclaims that race is "the most efficient instrument of social domination invented in the last 500 years," because it took shade and used it in a racial sense. Our observations were made based on literary, historical, and philosophical doctrines promulgated by the fiercest opponents of the equality of humans.

Europe not only invented a "Man," often referred to as "Universal Man," but someone that was disconnected from other humans, men and women, and had no soul, no emotion, no feeling, and no passion, except in the pursuit of personal greed and fame. This man was not a church, mosque, or synagogue Man; he was neither theocentric nor homo-centric. To characterize this form, this type, and claim it as *the* type that must be emulated is a strike against humanity. Our claim against this Man is not due to its anti-deity and de-god posture but on account of its dependence on the subjugation of women and the obliteration of African, First Nations, and Asian people. This concept of Universal Man was fraught with ignorance, pride, and assertion. Like the term "race," the term "Man" in whatever narrative it was employed as a model was pregnant with abuse, heresy, and brutality.

Zakiyyah Iman Jackson's book *Becoming Human: Matter and Meaning in an Antiblack World* (2020) is mostly wrapped in a detailed racial analysis of how people of European ancestry have marked Africans as different from human, thus seeking to move white people's thinking from Africans as animals to Africans as humans. There is much to discover in this book; however, our aim has been to demonstrate that the race paradigm is itself fraught with antihuman and consequently false realities. It does no real good to engage in this false reality because it is like going down into a mole hole that becomes a maze of its own geography. This racial thinking must be abandoned because we cannot argue that blackness is a disruption, for example, of the human when in fact the African people are the mothers and fathers of humanity. What seems to trap Jackson, although a very significant scholar, is her serious engagement with the tropes developed by white scholars of race and gender. These are intersections established by the racial regime created by hegemonic patriarchs. In places where she is able to displace and to critique race, Jackson succeeds in holding race at bay, but this is not sustained in her book because she still seeks to make race doctrines better, more equal, and just.

Our work does not disrupt the human; we say that the human has not been asserted under the centuries-old race regime. Patriarchy and hierarchy impose views that bifurcate, distort, and destroy. In our view, the Akan expression *onye onipa* ("she or he is human") relates closely to the idea that to be human is to be good. To be *onipa paa* is to be good; one cannot say this about someone who is bad. *Being* is primary, yet it is an ontological reality that must be seen in the light of collective reality. How could one truly be human without other humans?

What we call for is the erection of a new human, standing up in every society and in every village and city of the world, unburdened by the weight of white racial crimes and the guilt of those crimes. We write for the construction of an ethical human, never unnerved by the assaults of race, steady in the stream of life like the rocks in the mighty cataracts of the Nile, witness to the ages as they come and go—that is, a human freed from the insistence on blood distinctions that are unreal in rank, freed from human family quarrels brought on by religion, race, creed, and doctrines of domination. This is where we find a new regime comprising those who are emancipated mentally, liberated culturally, and freed of all colonial discursive moves and motivations. In effect, this has been from the beginning the work of Cheikh Anta Diop, Ana Monteiro Ferreira, Maulana Karenga, Vimbai Chivaura, Simphiwe Sesanti, Lehasa Moloi, and Joyce King, among others who have advanced the Afrocentric foundations for a new opening to humanity.

What Africans have always known is that race was an invented construction with no anatomical correlate like gender, for instance. The idea of race was used as a bludgeon around the world to divide people into civilized and uncivilized, believers in rationality and practitioners of emotion, those oriented to science and those oriented to superstition, and those who were aggressive and those who were easily defeated/taken over. Race unleashed an arrogant blueprint for imperialism and left the European ethos emboldened against all other people. America, Africa, Australia, Asia, and South America all fell before the sword of a marauding white race doctrine. Of course, one could see how this caused many whites to disregard the person of Africans, Native Americans, Australians, and Asians, criticizing our ways of knowing and practices of culture as subhuman. In effect, it is what Sylvia Wynter (2007) has called an "epistemological disregard" (p. 267).

The human as we have proposed is not the Christian/Muslim votarist of the church/mosque, or of any religion, but a new matrix of collective consciousness of the unity of the universe, the sibling relationship of all *Homo sapiens*, and the extensive bounty of living things that form a part of our precious environment. This should not be counted as a salute to the glorification of sameness but rather as an announcement of a new reality that subverts all dominations to the will of all other people. No one people and no one person rises above the masses in terms of quality of being, hence we claim an unbounded acceptance of individual will expressed collectively as the route to one status among humans. There are no *Homo sapiens* with superhuman status built into their genes; we are in effect one common humanity.

Wynter (2003) clearly argues that Europeans with their Christian ideology saw people as separate and different, to the extent that

> the enslaved peoples of Africa [were] transported across the Atlantic (classified as Negroes, negros/negras) into the physical referents of its reinvention of medieval Europe's Untrue Christian Other to its normative True Christian Self, as that of the Human Other to its new "descriptive statement" of the ostensibly only normal human, Man. (p. 265)

What Wynter knew was that the West did not view the African as a part of the category of "Man" in the same way as it viewed other Europeans. There was but one Man, and it was the Universal Man, respected in all fields for knowledge and leadership, represented from the 15th and 16th centuries by the European, not by the Yoruba, Zulu, Akan, Peul, Amhara, or Oromo. In fact, all humans not viewed as Man were relegated to museums, the place where Europeans could go and see what they were not while praising their constructed Scandinavian god that they were not Africans.

The idea of the museum as an institution that holds objects stolen from various people of the world is fundamentally one of the avenues through which Europeans travel the road of their idea of superiority. What Europe developed in the idea of a museum was spread throughout the world wherever the imperial Europeans conquered. People of Africa were called primitives, savages, and barbarians, and the museum would have shown these portrayals through the objects confiscated. Africans were called warlike, headhunters, and bloodthirsty as ways to reinforce their spectators' negative opinions of them. Of course, Africans never called themselves by such names and did not rank humans in such a fashion.

The Constituents of the Human

The ancient Africans of the Nile Valley, Kemet, Nubia, Kush, and Axum, whose cultures can be seen throughout the African continent, created a character-building experience that gave a model of human relationship that was later abandoned by those who invaded the continent with nefarious ideas. The ancient formula consisted of a demonstration of knowledge by the singer Odus, the Horoscopus, the Hierogrammat, the Stolistes, the Prophetes, and the Pastophori. According to Diodorus (Green, 2010), Herodotus (Asante, 2013), and Clement Pastophori of Alexander (Press, 2003), the singer Odus, holding a musical instrument, would demonstrate the ability to master two books of Djehuti, often called Hermes by the Greeks: One book was the songs of gods, and the other was the allotment of the king's life. The Horoscopus, carrying a sun dial or horologium and a palm leaf, the symbol of astronomy, demonstrates knowledge of Djehuti's book on astronomy. The Hierogrammat, with a feather in the hair and a book in the hand and a rectangular box with writing materials, demonstrates knowledge of the divine words *Mdw Ntr*, cosmography, geography, the topography of Kemet, and astronomy. The Stolistes brings the cubit of justice and the libation vessels to demonstrate the books of Djehuti that speak about the slaughter of animals. The Prophetes brings a jug of water and is followed by those with loaves of bread and demonstrates from the 10 books of Djehuti the laws concerning the deities, the deepest secrets of the study of the divine, the education of the priests, and the history of Egypt. The Pastophori shows knowledge of medical books and the diagnosis and treatment of diseases. Here is the emergence of human categories of knowledge based on what the scholars, priests, and students of the society had seen in their work. This is before the quadrivium and trivium; in fact, it is credible that the Greeks and Romans found their ideas of the categories of knowledge from these mysteries that were described by Africans centuries before the Greek civilization appeared.

REFLECTION ON A COMMON *SEBAYET* ("WISDOM")

How do humans achieve truth, wisdom, and justice? The learning through ancestral experiences, books, and experimentation can only put us on the road to humanity; it cannot give us truth, wisdom, and justice. We discover these qualities in our interactions with other humans, although it is necessary to overcome the severe constraints of racial indoctrination that leads to the racial ladder compromised with rankings. Without question, we must abandon the racial ladder as one would an instrument that is worn out, a dress that no longer covers the body, or shoes that are ragged and disgusting in appearance, because it cannot be recycled and will always restrain true humanity. The ladder is broken and useless, and never should have been proposed in the first place. Onward toward a new human discourse without collective ranking!

The end of education is to inquire with humility into the laws of nature to understand as much as possible the construction of the universe, the commonality of humanity, the source of light, and the relationship of one part to all other parts. This is the genuine meaning of education and the course of wisdom. There can be difference without othering. To be human is to manifest difference in many dimensions. However, othering exists when some humans label other humans as being outside of a particular construction of humanity. The others are outsiders without subject positions. Difference can be indicated in language, religion, accoutrements, and traditions, and we can speak of people as Russian, Islamic, Thai, and Zulu without denying the subject place of those people. By naming cohumans, we are in effect recognizing the intense and firm connection we have with all humans.

The quest of the human is to come as close as possible to the harmony of the natural order by subordinating the most perverse aspects of our thinking to the more positive sensibilities of seeking the best for ourselves. In this way, we journey toward the light for which we quest. We bring *Maaticity* into being!

Here, it might be well to note that African Egyptians were the first genuine priests in the history of the world, and they sought to fulfill the quest by understanding the role of the omnipotent sun in all human life. We cannot escape the clustering common to humanity. It is no wonder that the names of Ptah, Amen, Ra, and Atum are mentioned so early in human history as deities symbolized by the sun with its all-encompassing power. Throughout Africa, people have interpreted the Maatic understanding from the earliest times as a part of human heritage. For example, the Zulu Declaration, first promoted outside Africa by our late friend Jordan Ngubane, contains all of the values found in the ancient texts and oral traditions of African societies. The Zulu are Nguni-speaking people found in southeastern Africa, whose ancestral lands go back into the earliest millennia of human existence. Initiation into humanity consists, as it does in many African societies, of eternal commitments to fundamental relationships with neighbors and nature. The Zulu Declaration presented here is just one example of the African response to humanity (Nehusi, 2015).

The Zulu Declaration

I
I am
I am alive
I am conscious and aware
I am unique
I am who I say I am
I am the value of essence
I forever evolve inwardly and outwardly in response to the challenge of my nature
I am the face of humanity
The face of humanity is my face
I contemplate myself and see everything in me
I perceive; that which I perceive is form
Form is unchanging value
Value is eternal consciousness
Consciousness is that in which all things have their origin
It does not change; it exists from eternity to eternity
It is an infinite cluster of clusters of itself
It is forever evolving in response to the challenge of its nature
It is ultimate value
It is essence
The value metamorphoses into a phenomenon
Each phenomenon is a total of smaller forms
Phenomena form clusters to produce other phenomena
The cosmic order is an indefinite total of forms and phenomena
I am a phenomenon; I am a person
I am existence; I am consciousness
The infinity is a unity; it cannot be destroyed
I am a constituent of the unity
I cannot be destroyed

The infinity and I are inseparable
I cannot exist outside of the infinity
For there is no outside of it.
Everything is inside the infinity
Essence is the infinity
It is a Whole
It cannot be other than Whole; without me it cannot be Whole
Nothing can be added to or subtracted from the Whole
The infinity is alive
There is no death within it
There is life and perpetual agmination
That which is alive has purpose
Purpose is destiny
Perpetual evolution is the destiny of existence
Essence evolves in response to the challenge of its nature
The Law regulates evolution
It is a constituent of existence
It is the will of the Infinity
It is my will; it explains everything, for there are no mysteries
Mystery is the redoubt of the ignorant
Everything, everywhere evolves according to the Law
The Law is knowable
I cannot violate the Law no matter what I do
I incarnate the Law
Everything I do translates into action one section of the Law or the other
The processes of the Law are irreversible
Ultimate Absurdity is the attempt to invert the Law
The inversion of the Law is a cosmic cataclysm
It is Ultimate Criminality
I am the reconciler of all contradictions
The essence, the Law and I are together the Definite Agminate

Nothing can separate us
I live now
And shall live forever in existence
For I am essence
I am eternal; I am the secret that drives out all fear
Perpetual evolution is my destiny
I evolve forever, in response to the challenge of being human
I have a mind to light my path in the mazes of the cosmic order
The mind has many sides
It comprehends all things
It establishes my right to latitude; to be heard
It makes me feel at home in the cosmic order
My neighbor has a mind
It, also, comprehends all things
My neighbor and I have the same origins
We have the same life-experiences and a common destiny
We are the obverse and reverse sides of one entity
We are unchanging equals
We are faces which see themselves in each other
We are mutually fulfilling complements
We are simultaneously legitimate values
My neighbor's sorrow is my sorrow
His joy is my joy
He and I are mutually fulfilled when we stand by each other in moments of need
His survival is a precondition of my survival
That which is freely asked or freely given is love
Imposed love is a crime against humanity
I am sovereign of my life
My neighbor is sovereign of his life
Society is a collective sovereignty

It exists to ensure that my neighbor and I realize the promise of being human
I have no right to anything I deny my neighbor
I am all; all are me
I come from eternity
The present is a moment in eternity
I belong to the future
I can commit no greater crime than to frustrate life's purpose for my neighbor
Consensus is our guarantee of survival
I define myself in what I do to my neighbor.
No community has any right to prescribe the destiny for other communities
This universe I challenge a higher being than me to show
My knees do not quake when I contemplate my destiny
I know my way to eternity
I make obeisance to the million sides of the ciliate mind
The Eternal Person is Universal Man, Universal Woman, and Universal Child
I am a Universal Constant; I am a Cosmic Constant
I am All-in-One; I am One-in-All
I am the circle which encompasses infinity
I am the point that is the beginning of the circle
I am *umuntu*, the knower of all probabilities and possibilities
There is nothing I cannot know
There is no tyranny I cannot crush
The value of water is H2O; it lives from eternity to eternity
Nothing exists anywhere which can destroy it
I am who I am
I am not a creature; nothing can destroy me
I am the self-evolving value being; I live forever and ever

I am the phenomenon life-force
I am a person; a Ngubane; I am Ngogo Zabantu Nezezinkomo
I am a cluster; I am Skeletons of People and their Cattle
The cluster has vital elements
They are the center and core; the value of human being
The body, the aura, the law and essence
The law and essence are the environment in which I exist
I am a Ngubane; the Skeletons tell my history; they too define me
I am adequate; I have in me all I need to be the best I can be
I have contempt for that which is not freely given to me
Whoever wishes me good
Let that good go to him
Whoever wishes me to be a prince
Let him become a prince
Whoever wishes that I should die
Let his wish be his fate
For I want nothing to which I have no right
I am the servant of my ancestors
My father is the messenger of my ancestors
My ancestors are humanity
All I live for is to be the best that I can be
I do not prescribe destiny for my neighbor
My neighbor is myself in a different guise
Equals do not prescribe destiny for each other
They hold conversations of minds
They oppose ideas with counterideas
This, my ancestors told Shaka
Was the behavior of civilized men
They told him this from their fortress cave
Shaka forgot nothing
He carved everything on stone

A Zulu forgets nothing
I carve everything on stone
My adequacy makes me magnanimous
It makes me wise when strong and brave when weak
There are no frontiers I cannot cross
For I, the person, am my own challenge
Disease has no power over me when I know
I determine my health; I am what I want to bear
I see humanity on the high road to eternity
It marches along many routes
The Light in the person guides the march
It leads humankind along safer routes to a better future
My harmonized personality enables me to see my goal clearly
Every moment is a rebirth into a new dimension of being human
My duty is to guide the rebirth
I and I alone guide the rebirth
I outgrow the use of crutches
I face the challenge of being eternal
I align the cells in my body
I know each, by name
I am self-knowledge without end
That which I eat, drink or learn I convert into myself
I can afford to be humble; I am not afraid; I am adequate
That doctrine shall prevail which is afraid of the person
I reject all dogmas; they create disorder in my personality
I am the enemy of all dogma, for dogma is a prison of the mind
I am the egg in my mother's womb
I draw myself that which I need to evolve
Every moment of my life I evolve
For perpetual evolution is my destiny
I am the clot that extends itself into the person

Beyond Race: The Quest Back to Humanity

I am the person who extends himself into humanity
The mind of humanity comprehends infinity
Humanity is the blanket that covers my body; it is my flesh
It is the matrix in which I grow
It is the face of the infinity which sees itself
For essence knows itself
It knows its nature
It knows its destiny
It has within itself everything it desires
It is itself
It has no race and no color
The human value has no race and color
Each value metamorphoses in response to its environment
Behind each complexion is the environment
In each environment is a section of the Law
The Law is a Whole
It in itself is an infinite cluster of forces
Life is one of its components
The Law is another
So is Energy
So are others, seen, unseen, and incapable of being seen
My mandate is to know them all
To understand them all
I move from eternity to eternity to understand them
My sojourn on earth is a moment in my never-ending journey
My destiny is forever to respond to the call of the morrow
I have in me all I need to make the journey
I move from one dimension of being human to another
I move in proportion to the degree that I know
Knowledge is the key to the gates of every dimension
My title to the key is that I am human

I contemplate myself to discover myself
The key is my birthright
He is the enemy of humanity who denies me the key
For the key is the Law
I am born according to the Law
I live, grow and die according to it
My mother is the Law
My father is the Law
My relatives and neighbors are the Law
We are all bound together by the Law
My neighbors are mankind
Humankind is the Law
Phenomena divide and fuse according to the Law
Conflict is a dimension of the Law
Conflict is a moment of agmination
The stages of agmination are collision, disintegration, and fusion
Harmony and equilibrium are the fulfilment of the Law
The world is the Law
Everything is the Law; I am everything
I am the Law and my neighbor's will
I am the Law; I am a jewel of the cosmic order
The Law is my and my neighbor's will
I am a value; I have all the power to be what I want to be
There is glory in being human; in being a self-defining value
My name is Man; my name is Woman
I formed myself from my mandate
My mandate was the Law
I entered the earth as an act of will
I came to realise the promise of being human
To realize the glory of being human
To discover more satisfying dimensions of being a person

I am not alone; I have never been alone
I shall never be alone
For I am a cluster
I am Father–Mother
I am the cluster of phenomena which constitute me
I am Father–Mother–Child
I am the past, the present and the future
I have no beginning and no end
I am the geodesic circle in which Father and Mother merged
   to become Me
I extend myself into the child
I am the brick out of which society is built
I am the Eternal Person
In everything I think and do, I describe myself
I show how I face the challenge of being human
The Law is a component of *uqobo* itself
It has an infinite number of sections
The sections interact on each other
The interactions produce thought
The Law's interaction on itself in me produces thought
I translate thought into action
I create the world I desire through action
I evolve in response to the challenge of my nature
Thus, to evolve is life's purpose for me and my neighbor
We have in us everything we need to evolve
To discover satisfying dimensions of being human
To realize the promise of being persons
I am a witness of eternity
So is my neighbor
We are witnesses of what we are
We are living moments in eternity

I am a tiny component of *uqobo*, that is, itself
I am an element, a substance, and incarnation of it
I am an incarnation of the Law
I live in the Law; and the Law lives in me
It acts through me and fulfills itself freely
When I am ignorant, I disorganise the Law's interactions
I create disharmonies in my personality
I hurt my neighbour
I sow dissension in my environment
I frustrate life's purpose for humanity
I flee from the challenge of being human
I live in terror of myself
I plant terror into my neighbour's psyche
I terrorise all human beings
I move the world in cycles of conflict to catastrophe
I finally collapse midst the ruins I build
I rot in the prison of the mind I create
Passers-by note the stink
Here lies one who fled from the challenge of being human, they say
For I create my destiny in everything I do
I and I alone know this destiny
The challenge of being human is forever to explore myself
It is forever to understand my neighbour
Forever to reveal the power of the Definitive Agminate
The cosmic order is the seraskierate of the Definitive Agminate
I am the vizier of the seraskierate
The Law is my spectre
To know it is the challenge of being human
Forever to discover it is the promise of being human
Perfection is the continuing response to the ever-beckoning hand of the Law

Conquest forever distorts my personality
It is the aching wound that never heals
I listen to the call of the morrow
When to Ncome I shall return
When to Ulundi I shall return
I wait in the shadows of eternity
I wait for the day of rebirth into a satisfying destiny
I do not apologize for being human
I walk in humility in the presence of the person
If aught there is to worship, it is the person
To worship the person is to glorify myself
The person is real; he needs no oracles to interpret him
He has compassion in his bosom; the gods are capricious
They are crutches for all partisans for ignorance
The gods are trustees of my estate; I am the master
I grow in understanding
I outgrow the need for divine trustee; I stand on my feet
I march into the future on my terms
Nothing can strike terror into my heart
For I am essence of essence
I know every one of my cells
My mother taught me how to count them
My mother is all women; all women are my mother
I prostrate myself before all women
I cry out to them: Arise, mothers of the person
Lead your children along safer routes to a better future!
To all men I cry: Arise, fathers of the person
Create the world in which it will be no crime to be your children!
For all I desire is to realise the promise of being human
Good and evil are related
Either translates the Law into action

Virtue is knowledge and practice of the Law
Vice is ignorance of the Law
To know the Law is the glory of being human
It is *ukuba ngumuntu*, to be human
Perpetually to be responsible in *ukuba ngumuntu*
I have all I need forever to be responsible
For I am the source of all meaning, all value, and all authority
I build a Civilization in homage to the person
The highest points reached by other civilizations are in the sky
These zeniths are the levels from which I start building
I entered the earth to create order out of chaos
I recognize the person as my Light
I pay homage to the Light
The Light will prevail
For I know the heights from which they made me fall
I know the depths into which they thrust me
I know I shall prevail
For I am who I say I am
He has not been born who shall say he has conquered me!
   (Asante & Abarry, 1996, pp. 371–378)

Finally, we must understand that it is our acceptance of our common humanity that transcends the illusion of race because we have arrived at the African source from where we first met nature. The supreme human virtue is to admit the lies of the race paradigm, with its attendant descriptions of humanity, and accept the primacy of African origin at the beginning of history. This is humility. There is no struggle with the scientific and historical fact of our human existence with the African origins of humanity and civilization.

The perspective we present in *Being Human Being* is Afrocentric in the sense that it embarrasses all forms of what some call "superiorism" and debunks the insidious nature of "race" classifications and racial hierarchies by elevating cultural agency. We cannot move forward to Maaticity until we reposition the blackest-skinned woman, who is now at the bottom of the race paradigm, and recognize her as the mother of humanity.

There are ultimately no grounds for the particularistic European culture to assert itself as normative or universal. By what authority has Western culture or Islamic culture, or any culture, asserted its dominance by stigmatizing others as inferior? The bending of art, literature, science, and even theology to the cause of a racial categorization of superiors and inferiors, insiders and outsiders, white and black, and the advancing of heterosexual white male authorities, ritualistic demigods, and false ideologies of salvation have conspired to destroy not only the manipulators of societies but also all alternative views. We reject this construction as false, illusory in the end, and poisonous to the core in human relations. In fact, one cannot find Maaticity by following the path that has led to the destruction of good relationships with other humans, and the pollution of the air, ground, and water that we need for life. Maaticity does not bring the dehumanization, exploitation, and deception that we have seen in the patriarchal and hierarchal "racial" and "religious" regimes. All claims of universalism and normative authority that make some see themselves as humanists at the same time as they are dehumanizing others, that make them see themselves as worthy while others are deemed unworthy, must be rejected as we become human. *Khepera*, "the becoming," is what brings to life the transformation that we have sought in our own quest to dethrone all epistemic injustices and prevent the corruption of a new force for human freedom.

We must be prepared to accept a conscious agmination of humanity. The human is one, and all of the characteristics of being human are integrated into personhood. We commonly speak of the psychological, mental, physical, emotional, and spiritual aspects of the human, but in doing so, we are also ranking these various aspects. Most people think the mental is more important than the emotional because the perception is grounded in the ranking paradigm. Each human has all of these traits and therefore must be viewed as an agent, that is, an assertive being in the context of the environment, totally together and not as separate aspects of personhood.

Indeed, as Africologists, we establish the marker that we are human, and that is why we insist on the equality of difference and never on the ranking of humanity because of difference. Only in our particular needs because of capability must we prepare for uniqueness; otherwise, as Africans understood at the beginning of history, we are all traveling the same road from birth to death.

REFERENCES AND NOTES

Asante, M. K., & Abarry, A. (Eds.). (1996). *African intellectual heritage: A book of sources*. Temple University Press.

Baker, L. D. (1998). *From savage to Negro: Anthropology and the construction of race, 1896–1954*. University of California Press. https://doi.org/10.1525/9780520920194

Baker, L. D. (2011). *The anthropology of race*. http://people.duke.edu/~ldbaker/classes/anthropologyofrace/anthroOfrace11.pdf

Biko, B. S. (2002). *I write what I like: Selected writings*. University of Chicago Press. https://doi.org/10.7208/chicago/9780226368535.001.0001

Bondarenko, D. (2006). *Homoarchy as a principle of culture's organization: The 13th–19th centuries Benin Kingdom as a non-state supercomplex society*. Russian Academy of Sciences, Centre for Civilizational and Regional Studies and Institute for African Studies.

Bondarenko, D., & Korotayev, A. (2000). *The civilizational dimension*. URSS.

Butler, O. (1993). *Parable of the sower*. Four Walls Eight Windows.

Camus, A. (1948). *The plague*. (S. Gilbert, Trans.). Hamish Hamilton.

Dunaway, L. S. (1925). *What a preacher saw through a keyhole in Arkansas*. Parke-Harper.

Fanon, F. (2001). *The wretched of the earth* (C. Farrington, Trans.). Penguin. (Original work published 1961)

Fanon, F. (2008). *Black skin, white* masks (R. Philcox, Trans.). Grove Atlantic. (Original work published 1952)

Ferreira, A. M. (2015). *The demise of the inhuman: Afrocentricity, modernism and postmodernism.* SUNY Press.

Foucault, M. (1990). *The history of sexuality.* Vintage.

Galeano, E. (1997). *Open veins of Latin America: Five centuries of the pillage of a continent.* Monthly Review Press. (Original work published 1971)

Green, P. (Trans.). (2010). *Diodorus Siculus, Books 11–12.37.1: Greek history, 480–431 BC—the alternative version.* University of Texas Press.

Harrison, V. I., & D'Angelo, K. P. (2021). *Do right by me: Learning to raise black children in white spaces.* Temple University Press.

Herodotus. (2013). *Histories, Book II* (M. K. Asante, Introduction). In *Herodotus on Egypt.* Ramses.

Horsman, R. (1981). *Race and manifest destiny: The origins of American racial Anglo-Saxonism.* Harvard University Press.

Jackson, Z. I. (2020). *Becoming human: Matter and meaning in an antiblack world.* New York University Press. https://doi.org/10.18574/nyu/9781479890040.001.0001

Kaplan, S. (1991). The miscegenation issue in the election of 1864. In *American studies in black and white: Selected essays, 1949–1989* (pp. 47–100). University of Massachusetts Press.

Kendi, I. X. (2019). *How to be an antiracist.* Random House.

Kenyatta, J. (1962). *Facing Mount Kenya.* Vintage.

Las Casas, B. de. (1992). *A short account of the destruction of the Indies.* Penguin. (Original work published 1552)

Nehusi, K. S. K. (2015). *Libation: An Afrikan ritual of heritage in the circle of life.* University Press of America.

Nhemachena, A., Hlabangane, N., & Kaundjua, M. B. (2020). Relationality or hospitality in twenty-first century research? Big data, Internet of Things and the resilience of coloniality in Africa. *Modern Africa: Politics, History and Society, 8*(1), 105–139. https://doi.org/10.26806/modafr.v8i1.278

Orwell, G. (1949). *1984.* Secker & Warburg.

Press, G. A. (2003). *Development of the idea of history in antiquity.* McGill-Queen's Press.

Quijano, A. (2000). Quétal Raza! [What a people!]. *International Latin American Studies Review,* No. 1, 11–13.

Stockley, G., Mitchell, B. K., & Lancaster, G. (2020). *Blood in their eyes: The Elaine massacre of 1919.* University of Arkansas Press. https://doi.org/10.2307/j.ctv105b952

Thompson, R. F. (1984). *Flash of the spirit: African and Afro-American art and philosophy.* Vintage.

Wynter, S. (2003). Unsettling the coloniality of being/power/truth/freedom towards the human, after man, its overrepresentation: An argument. *New Centennial Review, 3*(3), 257–337. https://doi.org/10.1353/ncr.2004.0015

Yacovone, D. (2020, September 4). How textbooks taught white supremacy. *Harvard Gazette.* https://news.harvard.edu/gazette/story/2020/09/harvard-historian-examines-how-textbooks-taught-white-supremacy/

Index

Abdullah, Melina, 76, 125
Abdulrajeem, Issam, 107
Abraham Flexner Report, 134
Abrahamic tradition, 67
Achebe, Chinua, 119, 120
Africa, 5, 8, 15-17, 36, 76–84, 141, 176, 194,
African Matriarchal Foundations: The Igbo Case, 24
African Womanism, 33
Afrikan Mothers: Bearers of Culture, Makers of Social Change, 3
Afro-Germans, 102
Ali, Muhammad, 125
Amadiume, Ifi, 24
Ambedkar, Babasaheb, 27, 74
American Indian Holocaust and Survival, 62
Amharas, 104, 105
Ani, Marimba, 63
Arab, 14, 24, 31, 67, 78, 92, 107, 157
Aristotle, 102, 103
Arkansas Gazette, 162
Aryans, 43, 67, 72, 73, 110, 171, 176
Asante, Molefi Kete, 140
Asar, 72
Aset, 72
A Soldier's Play, 120
Australia, 44, 54, 61, 108, 127, 154
Australoid, 111
Azumah, J. A, 68, 71, 72
Bachofen, J. J., 22
Baker, Lee D., 103, 185
Balais, 74, 75
Baldwin, James, 97
Barthes, Roland, 137
Battle of Canal Street, 164

Beauvoir, Simone de, 30
Bedouin race, 53
Bell, Derrick, 5
Ben-Levi, A. J., 66, 73
Berlin Conference of 1884–1885, 101
Between the World and Me, 5
Biko, Bantu Stephen, 183
Black Skin, White Masks, 182
Black-skinned African women, 76
Blay, Yaba, 147
Black Lives Matter (BLM), 107
Bondarenko, Dmitri, 166
Brahmin, 25, 26, 31, 72, 73, 74, 75, 76
Brown v. Topeka Board of Education, 101
Butler, Octavia, 171
Bynum, Edward Bruce, 65
Camus, Albert, 138, 171
Capoid, 111
Caste: The Origins of Our Discontents, 3
Castration, 30, 68, 69, 70, 72, 74, 184
Caucasoid, 62, 110
Champollion, 80
Chaney, James, 142
Chinweizu, 55, 56, 62
Chivanhu, 172, 173
Chivaura, Vimbai, 190
Chomsky, Noam, 140
Christian consciousness, 154
ciKam, 78
Civil War, 96, 99, 132, 144, 164
Civilization or Barbarism: An Authentic Anthropology, 8
Coates, Ta-Nehisi, 5, 142
Cole, Johnetta Betsch, 125, 126
Conrad, Joseph, 119, 120
Consort of the Two Ladies, 25
Constantine, 45, 46

Coon, Carleton Stevens, 111
Council of Nicea, 45, 46
COVID-19, 2, 13
Crenshaw, Kimberlé, 182
Crescent City White League, 164
Critical race theory, 182
Dalits, 26, 29, 73, 74, 75, 176, 188
Darwin, Charles, 33, 59, 60, 61, 70, 101, 110, 119
Dasa, 72, 73
Davis, Angela, 76, 125
Davis, David Brion, 63, 64
Decolonial, 170, 181, 186
Demagogue, 14, 96, 101, 124, 125, 126
Derrida, Jacques, 137, 138, 139, 140
Differentiation, 6, 8, 66
Diopian, 8, 94
Djehuti, 192, 193
DNA, 7, 94
Dobzhansky, Theodore, 111, 112
Dove, Nah, 3, 7, 9, 20, 29, 36, 37, 57, 65, 93
Dred Scott, 99
Dred Scott v. Sandford, 128
Dunaway, Sharpe, 162
Egyptian, 77, 83, 91–92, 113, 172
Emerson, John, 99
Engels, Frederick, 22
Episteme, 14, 15, 16, 17, 29, 30, 32, 34, 37, 38, 39, 40, 63, 170, 176
Ethiopian race, 53
Eugenius IV, 154
European Crusades, 8, 154
Faces at the Bottom of the Well, 5
Facing South to Africa, 140
Fanon, Frantz, 64, 133, 181, 182
Feagin, Joseph, 14, 142 143, 144
Ferreira, Ana Monteiro, 175, 190
Fifteenth Amendment, 129
Film, 132, 133, 142
Firmin, Anténor, 109, 110
First Nations, 38, 62, 63, 108, 110, 127, 128, 155, 158, 160, 172, 176, 189
Flexner, Abraham, 135

Florisbad Skull, 93
Floyd, George, 2, 16, 30, 35, 107, 128, 142
Foucault, Michel, 137, 138, 140, 159
Fourteenth Amendment, 100, 129
From Savage to Negro: Anthropology and the Construction of Race, 1896–1954, 103
Fulani, 79, 105
Fuller, Charles, 120, 121, 122, 123, 124
Galeano, Eduardo, 158
Galton, Francis, 101
Gandhi, Mohandas Karamchand, 75
General El As, 79, 92
Gobineau, J. A. Comte de, 109, 110
Goodman, Andrew, 142
Gordon, Vivian, 126
Gould, Stephen Jay, 35, 59, 60, 103
Great Deluge, 67
Griffith, D. W., 132, 133
Haida First Nation, 44
Haitian Revolution, 71
Harlan, John Marshall, 101
Hausa, 79, 105
Heart of Darkness, 148
Hefny, Mostafa, 89, 92
Heidegger, Martin, 136
Hercules, 172
Herodotus, 6, 80, 81, 102, 172, 192
Heterarchy, 166, 167
Hierarchy, 6, 13–18, 22, 28, 32, 40, 47, 55, 76, 105, 133, 175
Hierogrammat, 192
Hindu, 27, 72, 74, 75, 76, 98, 108
Histories, 6, 102, 172
Hitler, Adolf, 102, 137, 155
Homo antecessor, 93
Homo erectus, 93
Homo sapiens, 5, 7–9, 20, 21, 46, 61, 81, 93, 94, 101, 106, 107, 111, 157, 172, 175, 176, 191
Homo sapiens sapiens, 94, 172
Homoarchy, 166, 167
Homosexual, 71, 102
Horoscopus, 192

Index

House of Humanity, 169, 174, 175, 176
House of Race, 168, 169, 174, 175, 176
Human Genome Project, 94
I Write What I Like, 183
Jackson, Zakiyyah Iman, 189
James, LeBron, 125
January 6, 2021, 13, 125, 153, 163, 170
Jebel Irhoud, 93
Jews, 92, 104, 110, 138, 155
Johnson, Andrew, 164
Kaepernick, Colin, 76, 125
Karenga, Maulana, 126, 190
Kemet, 25, 31, 34, 41, 71, 78–79, 84, 103, 172, 192
Kendi, Ibram, 1, 96, 114, 130
Khougli, Reem, 107
Killers of the Dream, 95, 115
King, Joyce, 190
Knox, Robert, 60–61
Korotayev, Andrey, 166
Kshatriyas, 73
Kushites, 72–73, 78
Lacan, Jacques, 137
Lacks, Henrietta, 135–136
Laws of Manu, 25, 27, 73
Lee, Spike, 126
Lenin, Vladimir, 136
Levinas, Emmanuel, 30
Lévi-Strauss, Claude, 137
Lewis, Bernard, 53, 66, 76–78, 86
Linnaeus, Carl, 35, 59, 93
Lorde, Audre, 29–30
Ma'at, 9, 15, 22, 38, 41, 82, 126, 172–173, 183
Maafa, 63, 84
Maatian principles, 178
Maaticity, 9–10, 183, 194, 207
Marx, Karl, 20, 64, 126, 136,
McLuhan, Marshall, 117–118
Melanin, 16–18, 39, 54, 65–66, 82, 178
Missouri Supreme Court, 99
Moloi, Lehasa, 190,
Mongoloid, 111
Montagu, Ashley, 111–112

Morgan, Lewis Henry, 22
Morocco, 93
Nash, Diane, 125
Nazi, 102, 132, 136, 155, 165
Negritude, 136
Negro Ensemble Company, 121
Negroid, 60, 78, 110
New Orleans Separate Car Act of 1890, 100–101
Ngubane, Jordan, 56, 194
Nhemachena, Artwell, 172
Nietzsche, Friedrich, 138
Noah, 67, 72
No More Women Oppression, 107
Obenga, Theophile, 84
Office of Budget Management, 91
Omo Kibish I, 93, 113
On the Origin of Species by Means of Natural Selection, or the Preservation of Favoured Races in the Struggle for Life, 110
Onwuachi-Willig, Angela, 95
Orientalism, 77
Oromo, 105, 191
Orwell, George, 209
Oyěwùmí, Oyèrónkẹ́, 23, 28, 34
Parable of the Sower, 171
Pastophori, 192, 193
Patriarchy, 6, 13–47, 64, 103, 117, 141, 175
Pelosi, Nancy, 13
Pence, Mike, 13, 50
People of color, 106, 143
Peraa Senursert III, 78
Peraat Neith-Hotep, 25
Persian race, 53
Petty, William, 60
Plato, 103
Plessy, Homer, 100
Plural societies, 106
Politics, 102
Pope Clement VI, 56
Prince Henry, 64
Prophetes, 192, 193

Quijano, Aníbal, 188
Race and Color in Islam, 76
Race and Slavery in the Middle East: An Historical Enquiry, 77
Racial ladder, 2, 4, 11, 57–66
Racism, 1, 3, 11, 58, 64, 70, 88, 113, 117–147
Racism in American Public Life, 125, 149
Rice, Tamir, 156
Riefenstahl, Leni, 132
Rig Veda, 40, 72, 76
Rittenhouse, Kyle, 118, 141, 149
Robinson, Jackie, 125
Romas, 102
Rousseau, Jean-Jacques, 138
Rushton, Philippe, 70, 87
Said, Edward, 77
Salih, Zeinab Mohammed, 106
Sankofa, 28, 51, 179
Sartre, Jean-Paul, 136, 137
Schwaller de Lubicz, René, 136
Schwerner, Michael, 142
Science, 4, 5, 57, 93, 111, 163
Sebayet, 15, 38, 193–194
Sesanti, Simphiwe, 190
Shem, Ham, Japheth, 67, 154, 157
Shujaa, Mwalimu, 54, 87
Slavs, 110, 171
Smith, Lillian, 95
Socrates, 103
Sousa Santos, Boaventura de, 140
Southwest Asian culture, 66–72
Stamped From the Beginning: The Definitive History of Racist Ideas in America, 3, 96, 114
Stewart, Maria, 125
Stolistes, 192
Stop First Nations Deaths in Custody, 108
Subgenation: The Theory of the Normal Relation of the Races: An Answer to "Miscegenation", 168
Sudanese women, 31, 71
Sudra, 26, 31, 73–74
Taney, Roger, 128

Taylor, Breonna, 30, 35, 151
Tedla, Eleni, 28
The African Origin of Civilization, 7, 36, 84
"The Annihilation of Caste", 74, 84
The Birth of a Nation, 132
The Demise of the Inhuman: Afrocentricity, Modernism, and Postmodernism, 175
The Elaine Massacre of 1919, 162
The Miseducation of the Negro, 29
The Mismeasure of Man, 103
The New Orleans Massacre of 1866, 164
The New York Times, 95
The Order of Things, 137
The Plague, 171
The Wretched of the Earth, 208
Things Fall Apart, 182
Third Reich, 155, 171
Thirteenth Amendment, 129
Thompson, Robert Farris, 187
Thornton, Russell, 62, 69, 88
Tigrean, 105
Tolmacheva, Marina, 70, 88
Triumph of the Will, 132
U.S. Census, 92, 112
U.S. Supreme Court, 9, 100, 128
Ubuntu, 172, 173
Universal Man, 188, 191, 198
University of Edinburgh, 61
Vaisyas, 73
Van Evrie, John H., 167–168
Varnas, 73
Volney, Count, 80, 83, 88, 178
Ward, Douglas Turner, 121
Weber, Shirley, 126
Weekly Day Book, 167
West, Cornel, 126
Wilkerson, Isabel, 3, 11
Woodson, Carter G., 29
Wynter, Sylvia, 190, 191
X, Malcolm, 76
Yacovone, Donald, 159, 210
Zanj, 31, 70, 71
Zulu Declaration, 194, 195

Other Titles from Universal Write Publications

Revolutionary Pedagogy, Expanded Edition
Molefi Kete Asante

The Afrocentric School [a blueprint]
Nah Dove

400 Years of Witnessing
Molefi Kete Asante

We Will Tell Our Own Story: The Lions of Africa Speak
Adebayo C. Akomolafe, Molefi Kete Asante, Augustine Nwoye

The Precarious Center, or When Will the African Narrative Hold?
Molefi Kete Asante

African Pyramids of Knowledge
Molefi Kete Asante

Visit UWPBooks.com
or find it at your favorite online bookstores